Making it Public

Evidence and Action against Privatisation

Dexter Whitfield

Pluto Press

First published in 1983 by Pluto Press Limited,
The Works, 105a Torriano Avenue,
London NW5 2RX

British Library Cataloguing in Publication Data
Whitfield, Dexter
Making it public, evidence and action against privatisation.
1. Government ownership—Great Britain
I. Title
354.4107'2   HD4145
ISBN 0-86104-509-2

Cover designed by Clive Challis A Gr R
Cover photograph: Crispin Hughes/Photo Co-op
Computerset by Promenade Graphics Limited
Block 23a Lansdown Industrial Estate, Cheltenham GL51 8PL
Printed and bound in Great Britain
by Richard Clay (The Chaucer Press) Limited, Bungay, Suffolk

Contents

Acknowledgements

This book grew out of two education packs on privatisation which Services to Community Action and Tenants (SCAT) produced with NUPE's London Division and National Office. I have written it to explain more fully the what, why and how of privatisation and to widen the debate about strategies to shop stewards in all public sector unions. It is addressed equally to tenants' campaigns, women's organisations, unemployed action groups and other labour movement organisations representing both workers and users of services.

I am indebted to shop stewards around the country who, faced with the threat of privatisation, have shared information, ideas and experience in educationals and meetings. Sally Watson assisted, encouraged and gave me love and comradeship throughout. I am very grateful to Jim Cornelius, Roger Critchley, Bob Evans, Dave Hall, John Harrison, Tom Snow, Stuart Speedon and Jenny Webber who read and commented on the draft. I hope to have done justice to their comments and ideas.

I would also like to thank Christina Weller who helped with the typing, and the American Federation of State, County and Municipal Employees and the Service Employees International Union for material on contracting out in America.

To Lewis and Sara
and all other kids.
They face a grim future unless we all fight for
workers' and users' control of public services.

1.

Privatisation: the Threat

For some, privatisation is big business. As you read this, solicitors and estate agents are busy preparing documents for the sale of council houses, a National Health Service nursing home, school playing fields and other publicly owned 'ripe for development' sites. Or maybe they're counting their commission.

City stockbrokers and bankers are gambling on the Stock Exchange indicators. Should they sell shares in British Aerospace and Amersham International now? Or will share prices rise still further?

At a regular meeting of a right-wing pressure group in a West End hotel, businesspeople, academics and two Tory MPs discuss the complete privatisation of schooling and state pension schemes.

Meanwhile, on a council estate in South London, a group of refuse collectors returns home after an eight-hour day humping bins. They're exhausted. Another worker was fired today for arguing with the company manager about the organisation of the round. There's no trade union, no pension, and nothing if you are ill for more than a few weeks.

A neighbour sets out to work the nightshift for a contractor cleaning a nearby hospital—tired from a long argument with the council, who sent in a private builder to repair the roof. The tenant's got to foot half the bill. And what happens if the leaking roof makes the kids ill? The local hospital is private and the fees are far in excess of what the insurance pays for.

Unemployed people meet to campaign against new charges at the sports centre. The council sold it recently, and its multinational owners have abandoned concessionary rates.

Privatisation is more than asset stripping the public sector. It is a comprehensive strategy for permanently restructuring the welfare state and public services in the interests of capital. This is on such a scale that, by 1990, we could be looking back at the welfare state as simply a bygone period in history. We will be relying on multinational contractors for 'cradle to grave' services.

Restructuring can only be implemented by a sustained attack on public services and the trade union movement. For workers and users it means more job losses and wage cuts, working harder for longer hours, with worse conditions. It means paying more for poorer services. Profitability, not need, will dictate the provision of services. Meeting needs will be the responsibility of the individual. Collective responsibility, provision and control will be a thing of the past. Tory propaganda about more choice, greater flexibility and increased efficiency hides the stark reality of third-rate health care, third-rate education and third-rate social services for working-class people.

The struggle ahead

Another five years of Tory rule will make privatisation achieved to date pale into insignificance. No part of the public sector will escape. There will be no sanctuary in Labour-controlled councils. New laws will force them to hive-off most local government services to contractors.

Nobody should underestimate the personal consequences of continued privatisation. The Tories talk about 'rolling back the frontiers of the state'. What this means is a return to nineteenth-century Britain, with few or weak unions, and services such as health, housing, education and social services dependent on charity. California, the richest state in the USA, has recently opened a workhouse. It is cheaper than paying unemployment and welfare benefits.

Capitalism survives by constantly expanding and seeking new markets. In a period of prolonged recession, capital seeks new sources of profit. This must be viewed historically as a series of phases. These phases overlap and have occurred at different times in different services.

The first phase was the private provision of services and infrastructure such as roads and railways. They were concentrated in rich and middle-class neighbourhoods.

Then, with the municipal socialism of the late nineteenth century, came a phase of increasing state intervention. The state made direct provision of services, and effectively competed against private companies. Services were now extended to working-class areas. It was also argued that the state, exempt from the wasteful competition that existed between firms, could provide them at less cost. In addition, the trade union movement demanded controls on companies to protect people from the more brutal effects of market forces.

In the third phase, between 1919 and 1948, the state took full responsibility for many services. This was partly as a result of the failure of the private market. It was also due to strikes, riots and the demands of the labour movement for comprehensive public services. Industry wanted a national transport and communications and energy supply, but companies running many services had failed to invest and rationalise competition.

In the following period, the state both ran and managed services, becoming responsible for providing a healthy, educated and well-housed workforce. Services increased, particularly during the 1950s and 1960s, when the world economy was expanding and the trade union movement solid. Capital also gained from guaranteed markets and the financing and building of new facilities.

We have now entered a period of contraction. Capital needs to regain control over the profitable parts of services and a greater share of the work supplying public services in order to maintain profitability, and this is the key to understanding the whole drift of Tory policy.

The re-election of a Labour government would not be a complete solution. Simply to reverse all the privatisation legislation would take months of parliamentary time. Tory-controlled local authorities would continue to privatise local services. It should also be remembered that the previous Labour government sold £570 million worth of shares in BP, made savage cuts in public spending between 1975 and '79, and allowed Tory-controlled councils to sell thousands of council houses.

Renationalisation and the expulsion of contractors from local government would be just the first steps. They must be backed by an overall strategy to fight for improved public services, restructured on working-class terms under workers' and users' control. Recent resistance, though limited in ambition, shows that privatisation *can* be fought. Sheffield and Leeds councils have expanded their Direct Labour Organisations. Joint action in Bury prevented contractors taking over the Public Services Department.

Work has been clawed back from contractors in Camden, Hounslow and Croydon. Several coach operators have pulled out of competing with the National Bus Company.

Privatisation has drastic consequences for the labour movement. But it does present us with certain challenges and opportunities.

First, it gives a platform on which to campaign for improvements in public services—privatisation cannot be fought by defensive action alone.

Second, it pushes workers and users to develop much stronger working relationships and to build unity between public sector unions, tenants' groups, trades councils and other labour movement organisations.

Third, it challenges traditional ideas about trade unionism. Action cannot be limited to pay and conditions but must extend to the control, quality and range of service.

Fourth, it challenges our lack of control over the use of our savings and pensions contributions. These funds are currently used to buy shares and to build new private hospitals.

The rest of this book falls into two broad parts. The first part shows what privatisation is occurring, how it is justified, who benefits and who pays. The second argues the case for public services and develops strategies to defend and improve them. It is broken down into chapters in the following way.

Chapter 2 describes six different types of privatisation and shows its scale in local government, the NHS, nationalised industries, universities and government departments. It also describes the different methods the government has used to sell assets and transfer work to the private sector. Finally, it explains why the government is so committed to privatisation and what it hopes to achieve.

Chapter 3 exposes several myths created by Tory propaganda. It shows that privatisation doesn't redistribute wealth, and that money is actually wasted by changing the ownership of services. Chapter 4 examines the network of right-wing organisations, employers' federations, companies and consultants clamouring for more privatisation.

Chapter 5 examines the harsh effects of privatisation on workers, users and services. It draws on evidence from the USA, where contractors and consultants have a stronger foothold in Federal, State and local government.

Chapter 6 looks at the origins of services in the nineteenth century and shows why they were eventually taken over by the state. It then examines the role of the public sector in the economy today and the inbuilt contradictions of the welfare state in a capitalist economy.

Chapter 7 draws out the lessons from recent campaigns against privatisation and spending cuts. It argues that a new political strategy for the public services is urgently needed by the labour movement. It suggests the basic ingredients of that strategy.

Chapter 8 outlines a seven-point plan for activists in areas immediately and directly affected by plans for privatisation.

2.

Privatising the Parts Others Can't Reach

The government is using extensive powers to enforce privatisation. This is matched only by its determination to create the ideological and physical conditions that will guarantee a 'demand' for privatisation. This chapter looks at how this is done.

Originally used to describe the resale of nationalised industries to the private sector, privatisation now includes the sale and transfer of work and responsibilities throughout a wide range of public services and assets. It affects us as workers and/or as users. It threatens our daily use of transport, telephones, and services such as health, housing and education. Understanding Tory strategy is the first step towards developing counter measures. This chapter identifies six forms of privatisation and gives details of where it has occurred, or is planned.

 Transferring work and hiring private contractors

Increasingly, public bodies occupy a supervisory role in the running of key services. The work itself is done by private contractors. The attractions for private capital are obvious: services are big business. Each year, the NHS and local authorities spend over £30,000 million. Refuse collection alone accounts for some £500 million, and a further £3,000 million goes on NHS provision of ancillary services, such as catering, laundry and cleaning.

Most services and adminstration are threatened. Few public sector jobs are safe, and no type of job is sacrosanct. Manual, administrative, professional, technical and management staff are all in jeopardy. For even though the present level of contracting out of services is relatively low, it is on the increase *across a broad area of work*. Recent surveys by management consultants Coopers and Lybrand and by Conservative Central Office show that various authorities now use private firms for services ranging from sewer maintenance to health care. But some services have been riddled with contractors for years. For example much council housing has been designed, built and repaired by private firms. A few London boroughs tried to use contractors for refuse collection in the 1960s but the work soon reverted back to the local authorities because of increasing costs and difficulty in maintaining the quality of services.

The following sections list the effects of work transference in local authorities, the NHS, nationalised industries, government departments and further education.

Local authorities

* Services already privatised or threatened include architectural design, catering, school meals, refuse and cleansing, housing management and sales, building repair, parks and gardens, recreation and sports centres, building control, computer services, crematoria, transport and vehicle repair, legal and financial services, laundries, highway maintenance, and ambulance services.
* Controls on Direct Labour Organisations have been introduced to force the privatisation of more council house construction, improvement, repair and maintenance work, together with highway and sewer work.
* New schemes to force council tenants to carry out their own repairs or directly employ private builders are going through Parliament at the time of writing.
* Transport authorities are to be forced to consider private coach operators' bids for routes, special services, maintenance and catering. The Bill is currently being discussed in Parliament.
* Some parents have already been driven to repair and decorate their children's schools. The Assisted Places Scheme to finance children in private schools has been in operation from the early days of the Thatcher government. Contracting out of state education to allow parents to set up new private schools is on the agenda.
* An audit Commission has been set up to force more councils to use private accountancy firms for audits.
* Increasing use is being made of private nursing homes and voluntary agencies for care of children and the elderly.

National Health Service

* NHS hospitals have been directed by the DHSS to increase contracting out of cleaning, laundries, catering, building repair, non-emergency ambulances. An audit of several District Health Authorities by private firms is under way.
* Subcontracting of treatment and care of NHS patients to private hospitals is under discussion. A joint NHS–private hospital nurse training scheme is already in operation in London.

Nationalised industries

* British Steel plans to use contractors to carry out eight major areas of non-productive work—maintenance repairs, cleaning and substituting for absent steelworkers.
* British Rail is considering contracting out track maintenance. Railway workshops at Horwich and Shildon are threatened with closure because of increasing private ownership of wagons—by 1986, over 40 per cent of rail freight wagons could be in private hands.

Government departments

* The design of £2,000 millions' worth of major trunk road and motorways has been transferred to private consultants. Road Construction Units have been closed.
* The Property Services Agency has hived-off 5,250 jobs in architectural design, engineering maintenance, transport and vehicle repair, estates work building repair and maintenance, portering and removals. PSA may be turned into a commercial property company.
* The cleaning of government departments, the House of Commons, and other offices has been contracted out.
* Ministry of Defence insurance work, supplies and support services have been contracted out—600 jobs have already been lost.
* The Manpower Services Commission may privatise 69 skill centres and its 'temps' service and nurse-banks. Placements at Job Centres may be left to private firms' operations. The *Professional and Executive Register* may be at risk.
* The Department of Industry has contracted out security, typing, computer work, photographic and drawing office services, audit and accounts with the loss of 260 jobs to date.
* The Companies House business records service, the Central

Office of Information Film Unit, Ordnance Survey Maps and the Overseas Development Administration map section may all be hived-off.

* The Department of Health and Social Security has made employers responsible for Statutory Sick Pay. 3,500 jobs have been lost.

* The Science and the Victoria and Albert Museums, Kew Gardens, the Tower of London Armouries and various ancient monuments and historic buildings have been transferred to boards of trustees.

* The Megaw Report into Civil Service pay proposes using private consultants to determine pay limits.

* Up to 60,000 more civil service jobs are planned to go as result of departments contracting out cleaning, catering, building and ground maintenance, security, typing, vehicle maintenance and training.

* Private companies may take over management of £450 millions' worth of assets of the handicapped and insane.

Universities and colleges

* Cleaning, catering, portering, security, repair and maintenance and halls of residence are increasingly being contracted out.

 Selling state-owned companies and shares

The government accomplishes these sales in a number of ways. The first involves the conversion of nationalised industries into private companies with share capital. Just over half the shares are sold to private investors. The rest, retained for the present by the government, may be disposed of later in the same way. Subsidiary companies and those owned by the National Enterprise Board have been sold lock, stock and barrel directly to other companies. A third method is via a worker or management buy-out. Assets are often deliberately undervalued to enable privatisation to 'succeed'.

Details of actual and planned sales are given in the following sections.

Nationalised industries

* British Aerospace, Cable and Wireless, Amersham International, Britoil, and Associated British Ports have been converted into

private companies and shares sold to Stock Exchange speculators. British Shipbuilders, British Telecom and British Airways sales are planned. Rolls Royce may be sold later. The National Freight Corporation was sold to managers for £54 million.

* Nationalised industries' subsidiaries are also on the market: British Airways sold its College of Air Training and 47 light aircraft for £5.3 million; its profitable subsidiary International Aeradio was sold to Standard Telephone and Cables. BA Helicopters is for sale next. British Steel sold Vitaulic and its heavy engineering section Redpath Dorman Long. British Rail has sold its hovercraft service, laundries, 27 hotels and given away its Superbreak holiday venture. Sealink Ferries is also a candidate. British Gas has been forced to sell Wytch Farm oilfield worth £500 million—other assets have been transferred to four subsidiary companies for possible sale. Around 1,880 gas and electricity showrooms may also be sold. British Leyland may hive off Jaguar Cars, Land Rover and Unipart divisions.

* The British Technology Group (formerly the National Enterprise Board) has sold off several technology companies. NEB shares in Ferranti, ICL, Fairey and 24 other firms have been sold.

Government departments

* The £15 million Hydraulics Research Station, 91 Heavy Goods Vehicle Testing Stations, National Maritime Institute (270 jobs), 11 Royal Ordnance Factories (19,000 jobs) and Cattle Breeding Centre have been transferred to private ownership.

* The Department of Industry may sell its Computer Aided Design Centre—a leader in the application of computer techniques—to industrial design and manufacturing.

Selling public land and property

The Tory government has given council house tenants the right to buy their homes at up to 50 per cent discount. It's been dubbed the 'sale of the century' with good reason: so far, nearly 400,000 council houses have been sold at a total discount of over £2 billion. Any council reluctant to sell can be forced to do so under the 1980 Housing Act. In addition, entire housing estates are up for sale to private builders, again at knockdown prices. For example, Knowsley Council's Cantril Farm estate scheme guarantees 10 per cent profits to private contractors—the scheme itself is valued at £20 million.

Vacant public land is also up for grabs. So far, local authority registers have identified 90,000 acres—about 45,000 acres, or all the land with 'development potential', will be sold for development by property companies.

The following sections list actual and planned sales.

Local authorities

* 400,000 council and housing association houses were sold in the first three years of Tory rule. The right to buy is being extended to charitable housing associations. New 'Do it yourself Shared Ownership' schemes have been introduced for tenants moving towns.

* Glasgow, Liverpool and Edinburgh councils have sold whole estates at giveaway prices to private builders for conversion into luxury flats. Knowsley Council have sold the 3,312-dwelling Cantril Farm estate, built in the 1960s, to a consortium of Abbey National, Barclays Bank and Barratts for £8 million, less than half its real value. Hundreds of tenants will be displaced and the estate, renamed Stockbridge Village, will become mainly owner-occupied housing. Over 1,100 new houses will be built and nine tower blocks sold off.

* Local authorities have sold thousands of acres of housing land to builders and building societies. New Towns have sold housing, commercial and industrial sites.

* 2,370 acres of school playing fields and sports grounds are up for sale. Several colleges have been sold cheaply to private schools. Cambridgeshire County Council sold Wisbech Grammar School to an independent 'educational' trust.

* Housing associations are increasingly being pressured to build for sale rather than rental—including sheltered accommodation for the elderly.

* Up to 623 acres of London's Docklands are being sold to developers for private housing and commercial schemes—this includes 385 acres of public housing land.

* Grants are being made available to companies under the Derelict Land Act 1982 to encourage land reclamation by the private sector.

National Health Service

* Several NHS hospitals and nursing homes are being sold to

private health firms and developers.
* 3,325 acres of NHS land are up for sale.

Nationalised industries

* Nearly 20,000 acres of Forestry Commission land have already been sold.
* A number of large office blocks have been transferred by British Rail to British Rail Investment Ltd, a new company to act as a focal point for privatising the railway's assets.
* British Airways has sold its £3 million holding in London Penta Hotel.

Government departments

* 24 motorway service stations have already been sold.
* Land and buildings owned by the Property Services Agency have been hived-off.
* 90 homes on an RAF estate in Oxfordshire were sold to a property company.

Allowing firms to exploit public services

This is one of the more insidious forms of privatisation. The government baulks at the idea of the complete sale of transport, communications and energy systems. Instead, it does the next best thing—it allows companies to use the publicly provided network of cables and pipelines to sell their own services. It is unlikely that any of the proposals listed below would be economically feasible if they weren't given these concessions.

As a result of this misuse of the infrastructure, nationalised industries will be forced to operate more and more on the basis of profit rather than service. Catch 22 is that once any section becomes profitable it also becomes a candidate for privatisation.

The following sections give details of actual and planned schemes.

Local authorities

* The Thatcher government has been considering taking control of London Transport away from the GLC and privatising parts. Serious possibilities include hiving-off certain tube lines and/or allowing private coach operators to take over running bus routes.

National Health Service

* Full-time NHS Consultants and Community Physicians can now earn up to 10 per cent of their income from private health care.
* NHS hospitals are now allowed a greater number of pay beds.
* NHS laboratories and services are now being used for private patients, often without payment.

Nationalised industries

* Private firms can now generate and sell electricity via the national grid.
* Project Mercury (BP, Barclays Bank, Cable and Wireless) is setting up a new inter-city telephone network, using railway tracks, to compete for business calls with British Telecom.
* US oil companies in the North Sea are preparing to compete with British Gas for supplies to industrial users under the 1982 Oil and Gas (Enterprise) Act.
* Private firms can now sell phones to compete with British Telecom.
* Private coach operators are now allowed to compete with National Bus Company on profitable inter-city routes. Coach operators in Cardiff, Cumbria, Devon and Norfolk are competing with public transport buses on profitable routes.
* Private companies are now allowed to compete with the Post Office for certain mail traffic—including document exchanges, express mail, and the sale of postage stamps.

Universities and colleges

* Academic staff are increasingly under pressure to set up their own companies to exploit new products and techniques developed in university research facilities.

 Expanding private services

The government is encouraging the expansion of private hospitals, private schools and private transport services. It is also exploring ways in which private capital can be used to finance nationalised industries. Inevitably, private companies will concentrate on the profitable parts of services, leaving the public sector to provide the rest.

Government propaganda has not fallen on deaf ears. There are

13 private hospitals under construction and a further 45 are planned. Health insurance now covers four million people. Private schools and colleges will proliferate as a result of education vouchers, a scheme which entitles parents to a yearly voucher which they can use either to pay the cost of state education or in part-payment of private school fees.

The high costs of private facilities, coupled with cuts in public spending, are forcing more and more people to take care of children, the sick and the elderly at home. This form of privatisation claims women as its victims.

The following sections show the expansion of private services.

Local authorities

* New inner city grants are now closely linked to private finance and developers' schemes.
* Banks and building societies are now jointly financing housing for sale and rent with the Housing Corporation.
* The 1980 Housing Act made it easier for landlords to build more privately rented housing—Prudential, Barratts and other developers are currently setting up schemes.
* Student grants may be replaced by loans, and pilot schemes for education vouchers are to be introduced.
* Charges for lessons, textbooks and equipment in schools and colleges are being extended and raised substantially.

National Health Service

* The Government 'Think Tank' proposals to change the funding of the NHS to an insurance-based scheme and to expand private health is still under consideration.
* A series of government measures has been introduced to encourage private medicine, including the relaxation of restrictions on private hospital development, and the removal of tax charged on medical insurance.
* 'Partnership schemes' are being encouraged between NHS and private hospitals to 'share' health care responsibilities.
* There has been an expansion of private General Practitioner services, alcoholic and drug treatment centres, and community psychiatric centres.

Nationalised industries

* Private developers will be involved in redeveloping National Bus

Company terminals in city centres. Profits will be siphoned off instead of being used for subsidisation or improvement of other services.

* Private finance may be introduced into the new British Rail Victoria to Gatwick link.

* The government is considering developing a 'futures' market for NCB coal stocks.

* The merger of some BSC plant and a private steel firm to form Sheffield Forgemasters is merely one of several schemes for further privatising BSC currently under discussion.

* Martlesham Enterprises, British Telecom's research centre, has entered into a joint venture with financial institutions to market new products. Telecom Gold has been set up along similar lines to market an electronic mail service.

Government departments

* Major construction companies, together with financial institutions, may finance and build new trunk roads. The government would pay for usage or tolls will be introduced.

Hiving-off the future

Future benefits from research and technological advances are to be rooted in the private sector. To achieve this the Tories not only have to implement privatisation in the ways already described, but also to ensure that major inquiries, such as the Hunt Report on cable television and the Serpell Report on the future finances of British Rail, are dominated by free marketeers. Their narrow terms of reference guarantee that proposals are centred on commercial criteria.

Furthermore, business-oriented ideology will lead most people to expect profitable opportunities to be captured by the private sector.

The following sections list some examples of Tory ingenuity in this field.

Local authorities

* The Thatcher government intends future redevelopment and development of towns and cities to be firmly rooted in the private sector, with minimum state involvement. The Department of the Environment-sponsored Financial Institutions Group has set up

Inner City Enterprises (ICE) to seek out profitable projects and match up developers, builders and financial institutions, such as insurance companies, pension funds and building societies.

National Health Service

* The introduction of new techniques is increasingly concentrated within private hospitals. For example, test-tube baby clinics are no longer available in the NHS.

Nationalised industries

* The Hunt Report on cable television calls for private sector cable laying (worth £2,000 million alone), production and operation of stations, with minimal public sector control and involvement.
* The liberalisation of British Telecom services will lead to maximum exploitation of new technological developments by the private sector at the expense of the public sector.

Government departments

* The British Technology Group is to lose its automatic right to all inventions from public sector laboratories. In future, they will be developed mainly by the private sector.

How privatisation is implemented

The Tories' commitment to privatisation is indicated by the measures they will take to implement it. Their tactics include: new legislation and controls; the reorganisation and restriction of services; and radical policy reviews by the government's 'think tank', the Central Policy Review Staff.

Each year of Tory rule, legislation has been pushed through Parliament giving the government extensive powers to enforce privatisation. In 1980, the Housing Act and the Local Government Planning and Land Act gave council tenants the right to buy their homes and imposed controls on local authority Direct Labour Organisations (DLOs). In the same year, the British Aerospace Act and the Civil Aviation Act led to the sale of British Aerospace and changes in British Airways. Transport Acts in 1980, 1981 and 1983 provide for the sale of the National Freight Corporation, Heavy Goods Vehicle testing stations and British Rail subsidiaries; the reconstruction of the British Transport Docks Boards to form Associated British Ports; and the obligation on the metropolitan county Passenger Transport Executives and London Transport to allow tenders for routes and services, catering and maintenance.

The British Telecommunications Act 1981 and the Telecommunications Act 1983 cover the sale of Cable and Wireless and British Telecom and its subsidiaries. They give the government power to license other companies to run the telecommunications system and to suspend the Post Office monopoly. The sale of Britoil followed the Oil and Gas (Enterprise) Act 1982, which also gave the government powers to compel the British Gas Corporation to sell its assets, including showrooms, to private companies. In addition, the Act terminated the Corporation's rights as buyer of supplies from British gasfields and allowed private firms to sell gas using British Gas pipelines.

Other legislation extended privatisation. The Industry Act 1980 altered the powers and financing of the National Enterprise Board and led to the sale of shares in many companies. Shipbuilding and repair yards will be sold following the British Shipbuilders Act 1983. The Housing and Building Control Act 1983 extends the right to buy to housing association tenants and will privatise parts of the building control system.

As well as giving Ministers the power to compel the sale of assets and to suspend or close public services, most of these Acts also give private contractors rights of access to, and use of, public facilities.

Other Acts pave the way for privatisation by encouraging the adoption of more commercial attitudes. For example, the Competition Act 1980 extends the power of the Monopolies and Mergers Commission to conduct efficiency and performance reviews in nationalised industries. The Local Government Finance Act 1982 increases government control of local authority spending and imposes penalties for 'overspending'. Private auditors are empowered to investigate the 'economy, efficiency and effectiveness' of services and to determine 'value for money'.

As a sort of icing on the cake, the government issues Circulars instructing public bodies to increase privatisation. Early in 1983, a Department of Health and Social Security Circular instructed all health authorities substantially to increase contracting out of NHS domestic, catering and laundry work. The Department of the Environment's Circular 6/82 increased controls set by the Local Government Planning and Land Act 1980. The Act had forced DLOs to compete with at least three private contractors for all work above a certain limit (for example, highway work over £100,000 and all maintenance jobs over £10,000). The Circular halved the limit for highway work and 30 per cent of maintenance work under the limit had to go out to tender. However, contractors were still not satisfied, so, in December 1982, the government announced further limits. From October 1983, 60 per cent of both maintenance work under £10,000, and new construction work under £50,000 will go out to tender, together with one-third of highway work under the present limit.

The government does not increase the limits in line with inflation; instead it reduced them three times in as many years. This is simply a taste of what could happen if the Tories introduce similar legislation for other local government services.

Stacking the cards in private capital's favour is also shown by the planned abolition of the most recent Fair Wages Resolution (House of Commons 1946). Such resolutions, first passed in 1891, are designed to ensure that firms with government contracts provided wages and conditions on a par with collective agreements. Their abolition will help contractors to undercut public sector and other firms' wages. Over 300 local authority controls and requirements have been relaxed to make it easier for private firms to operate. The creation of twenty Enterprise Zones exempted firms from rates, Development Land Tax and training requirements and gave 100 per cent capital allowances on industrial and commercial buildings. At the same time the government lifted statutory obligations for local education authorities to provide school meals.

Privatisation means bonanza time for the consultants whose reports are used to prepare the ground. Incredibly, contractors have also been known to carry out efficiency studies—Oxfordshire County Council employed Grand Metropolitan to investigate their school meals service. Recommendations are nothing if not predictable. The Coopers and Lybrand study, commissioned by the Department of the Environment, advocated

> a fundamental review of local authority provision of allotments, smallholdings, markets, golf courses and laundries. Greater consideration should also be given to the hiving-off option for sports centres, cemeteries and crematoria, theatres and public halls and vehicle maintenance.

It also called for the 'hiving-off of some of the larger local authority research and intelligence units' and concluded that 'there is a strong case for authorities to review regularly each of their across-the-board services by testing the market through a tendering exercise, with a view to achieving economies'. 'Across-the-board services' include catering, ground maintenance, architectural design, legal and accounting services, payment of wages, security, insurance, advertising and design, printing, computing, office cleaning, maintenance and decoration, caretaking, gardening, building maintenance and window cleaning.

Local services, such as leisure and sports centres, also came in for scrutiny by Coopers and Lybrand. Local authorities' pricing policy was castigated as being 'incremental and strongly influenced by public service attitudes', and charges were 'too low on the mistaken assumption that the market will not bear a higher price'. The study concluded that services should be paid for in full 'to discourage frivolous consumption, prevent vandalism, reduce congestion, encourage efficiency (by making users appreciate the costs of the service) or avoid unfair competition'. Authorities should also 'ask themselves why should we provide this service at all?'

Reports such as these are used to coerce local authority workers to accept cuts in jobs and services. There is a danger that employers will institutionalise 'cost-cutting plans' as workers' plans. Trade unions will be forced constantly to produce 'savings plans' in order to retain the work within the public sector. This could develop quite rapidly. These 'plans' could be made to look progressive by including workers in the running of services when in reality they are a more sophisticated but manipulative cuts mechanism.

Other methods are employed to reorganise and restructure services. New companies and advisory boards are set up to sell off profitable parts and parcel work out to contractors. Design and sales currently carried out by the Ministry of Defence are to transfer to eleven Royal Ordnance factories. Already profitable, these factories should become even more 'attractive to buyers'. The 13-person Advisory Board to the Property Services Agency includes members from property groups Slough Estates, Taylor Woodrow, Ford and Stag Furniture. Not surprisingly, design, building repair, transport, vehicle and furniture workshops have been privatised.

The Tories' social policies have created the right conditions for public acceptance of privatisation. Longer hospital and housing waiting lists, coupled with tax relief on health insurance and mortgages, push people into the private sector. Generous discounts encourage council house sales just as higher charges for school meals, NHS prescriptions and council rents establish the idea of paying for services.

The Central Policy Review Staff has carried out three major policy reviews which, if implemented, will privatise large sections of the welfare state. The first, leaked to the press in September 1982, recommended replacing the NHS with private health insurance. It also called for an end to state funding of higher education and the use of market rates to establish the level of fees (currently about £12,000 for an average three year course). Loans and scholarships would replace student grants. The report, approved by the Treasury, envisaged massive savings from the privatisation of primary and secondary school education. Further savings were to come from keeping rises in social security payments—including pensions and supplementary benefits—below the level of inflation. Not surprisingly, their review of the £14 billion defence budget didn't yield any 'savings'. Despite protests from Tory 'wets', subsequent statements by Sir Geoffrey Howe and Leon Brittan, Chief Secretary to the Treasury, clearly indicate that these proposals have *not* been shelved.

The elimination of council housing was the subject of the second think tank report, leaked in December 1982. The plan is to turn council tenants into owner-occupiers by converting rent into mortgage repayments. Tenants would then be responsible for repairs and maintenance. There would be no new council housebuilding, except for sheltered accommodation. The paper evidently didn't deal with the problems of council flats nor those tenants receiving housing benefit.

Another leak, in February 1983, produced more in the same vein. Recommendations included tax changes to encourage women to stay at home to look after the elderly, disabled and unemployed; training children to use pocket money; handing over more personal social services to the private sector; and increasing individual responsibility for pensions.

These think tank proposals indicate the extreme measures the government will take to further privatisation.

Restructuring

Even where the Tories are not planning to privatise services (because of fear of working-class opposition or because public services undertake unprofitable work and provide some of the costly infra-structure unattractive to private firms) they plan to radically reshape them. This reshaping is dependent on privatisation in a number of ways.

(1) Increasing productivity and profitability

Workers often face cuts in wages, benefits and working conditions when they become employees of contractors rather than of public bodies. The threat of privatisation is used to encourage public employees to renegotiate the hard won gains of the last 35 years. Wage restraint imposed on the public sector then becomes a means of reducing wage claims from industrial workers. Since 1979, these tactics, coupled with mass unemployment, have en-abled the government to impose public sector pay settlements well below the rate of inflation.

The Tories also argue strongly that the rates of pay in central and local government should be determined by market forces. Hence the abandonment of pay comparability systems, such as the Clegg Commission, and the Megaw Report's proposed privatisa-tion of Civil Service pay studies. Fair Wages legislation and Wages Councils which set minimum wage levels are also to be scrapped. This is part of a wider plan of deregulation.

The shedding of jobs and changes in working practices are means of increasing productivity in both the public and private sectors. The propaganda about inefficiency is a red herring which disguises the real intention of forcing workers to accept lower earnings and worse conditions of employment in order to increase profitability. Workers lose what little control they had over their work.

Nor do worker buy-outs and co-operatives provide a solution. Evidence from the USA, where such buy-outs are more common, suggests that there's more to them than would at first appear. *The Economist* (13 March 1982) summed up some of the problems:

> In most instances, little shift to worker control or delegation of decision-making power actually followed the buy-outs, and worker ownership was sometimes more apparent than real. The impulse for it was invariably pragmatic: desperate work-ers bought jobs, accepting the possibility of a low return on their stakes. But the evidence suggests that worker purchases partly financed by the state can yield big productivity gains. First, manning (sic) cuts ensued, especially where strong trade unions had prevented them before. Second, active

worker initiatives raised product quality and cut production costs in several cases. Third, because participants chose to get involved in the process of negotiation to set up and pay for new enterprises, they responded, to a degree, to the incentive effects of ownership. This is not to say that industrial relations are always harmonious after a worker takeover. In America there has been a widespread tendency for conflict to re-emerge some months after the transition, and several experiments have quietly reverted to conventional ownership. A period of worker ownership is sometimes better understood as a temporary reorganising period. But even that has its benefits.

(2) Reducing other costs of production

Capital is constantly trying to reduce not only wages but all production costs. They include Corporation tax, local authority rates, National Insurance surcharge and energy costs. The CBI and other employers' organisations strongly support the government's strategy to privatise services and 'reduce the burden of the rates'. The CBI organised about 40 local campaigns to fight against increases in local authority rates in 1981–82. Cuts and changes in the pattern of public spending on public services and the welfare state mean, at least in theory, lower taxation and rates. Privatising services means that more services have to be paid for out of wages rather than by the government. It is unlikely that tax cuts will, except for people on high incomes, match the level of increased personal expenditure on services. The transfer of costs and responsibility for services from the state to the individual is yet another way of imposing wages cuts and decreasing costs to capital.

Capital expenditure on new housing, schools and hospitals is already cut to the bone; public spending can only be cut further by attacking labour costs. There are, of course, contradictions for capital. Different sectors often have conflicting demands. The construction industry depends on the public sector for 40 per cent of its work and has been hit hard by cuts in capital spending. It has consistently lobbied for increased public spending on new buildings and roads. Cleaning contractors, on the other hand, support the 'more cuts' lobby because it leads to more contracts.

(3) Opening up services and creating new markets for private sector exploitation

Firms are constantly looking for new areas of profitable work. The Tories came to power committed to increasing the private sector's share of work in the public services. The recession intensified this search, and the government's considerable assistance was more than welcome. But private capital wanted more. Not content with extra work and new markets, contractors also demanded that greater restriction be imposed on the public sector where it competed directly with the private sector.

(4) Reducing the strength of the trade union movement

This plays a central role in government strategy. The Tories believe the bargaining power of public sector unions prevents further wage cuts, in both private and public sectors, and hinders the implementation of employment legislation. Reducing the size of the public sector reduces the potential for conflict. Given that logic, it's a short step to privatisation and attempts to make public sector wages, conditions and benefits subject to the discipline of market forces. 'The more that public sector monopolies can be broken up into smaller competing entities, the more difficult it will be for a few unions to cause misery', is how the *Economist* (24 July 1982) described the strategy. Privatisation hits both jobs and union membership, because many firms are not unionised. It also forces changes within the unions because unions increasingly have members in both the public and private sector. The Tories hope that this will lead to more moderate trade union demands and policies.

The government is also using privatisation to try to create new but weaker bargaining groups. It also plans to extend the replacement of national bargaining (for example the abolition of the National Water Council) with regional and local bargaining in local government and other services. Each council would then negotiate locally and the Tories hope that pay and conditions would reflect local market conditions. By adopting divide and rule tactics it would be much more difficult to organise national pay campaigns. Other proposals being discussed include offering new review bodies, similar to that accepted by the Royal College of Nursing, in return for no-strike agreements in essential services like gas, electricity and water.

More stringent measures are being discussed. Writing in *The Banker* (April 1982) on public sector inflation, Tim Congdon, of brokers L. Messel and Co., argues that the solution

is for the government to strengthen its bullying position . . . So far UK governments have displayed a certain lack of imagination about the methods available. Recently, however,

Professor Meade has outlined some possibilities in his book on *Wage Fixing*. A union which failed to accept the arbitration of an independent pay tribunal and went on strike should, Meade suggests, be subject to certain sanctions. These might include the withdrawal of the right to redundancy money, the impounding of union funds and the payments of supplementary benefits only in the form of loans. Once a government began to go down this path, it is difficult to see where it might stop. In the last resort, it could evict recalcitrant strikers from council houses or end their right to state pensions.

(5) Creating the right ideology

This takes many forms. Its purpose is not only to encourage further privatisation but also to ensure that these changes are permanent and to minimise counter action by working-class people. To do this, Tory propaganda tries to create the illusion that workers actually have a stake in capitalism. Hence, tenants are given the opportunity to buy their council houses, and employees of nationalised firms may obtain a tiny percentage of the company's shares. In addition, as pension funds increase their shareholdings in companies, workers are led to believe that action against these companies, or demands for alternative investment strategies, will threaten their pensions. This is intended to create more conservative attitudes, to isolate workers further and to make them think before taking industrial action (see Chapter 3 for further discussions on these points).

Tory myths lower people's expectations about what the state should provide in an attempt to reduce demand for public services. The more caring, education and supervision which can be done by 'free' domestic labour in the home, the better. This is 'cost effective' and has the added bonus of reinforcing the ideology of family-based economics. The more standards of services decline, the more people are disenchanted and are forced to turn to private services. This allows the private sector to expand and to increase people's reliance on it. It also guarantees little resistance to further privatisation as there will be fewer people willing to defend public services.

Another essential ingredient of Tory propaganda is the encouragement of conflict and divisions within the working class. Workers have been led to believe that there is a fundamental difference of interest between trade unionists and non-unionists, between the employed and unemployed, between men and women, and between public sector workers and the users of services.

(6) Remoulding services to capital's needs
Increased emphasis is placed on public services meeting business and industry's needs. For example British Telecom is increasingly gearing the provision and charging of its telecommunications services towards business users. Companies are encouraging and forcing colleges and universities to tailor courses to the needs of industry at the expense of other courses.

(7) Increasing the power of the state to enforce these policies
Increased centralised control over local government, nationalised industries and other public bodies has ensured that Tory policies are actually implemented. Great collaboration with employers and increased spending on the police and defence have increased the power of the state to confront the labour movement and limit action against privatisation and other policies.

Future privatisation

Privatisation now lays the foundation for further privatisation later. Privatisation is a process which flourishes in, and helps to create and sustain, the particular ideological climate nurtured by the Tories. What may be safe today could well be considered suitable for privatisation soon. The present campaign has gathered rapid momentum only in the last two years. And the process of denationalising services and restructuring the welfare state cannot be achieved overnight.

For example, management are increasingly using volunteers in public services. Early in 1983, the government more than doubled its funding of projects organising groups of volunteers. This will bring the total to over 30,000 volunteers.

'Community care' can be an advance from incarceration in an institution, but it is used as a catch-all to aid Tory policies and spending cuts. Volunteers, usually women, are increasingly used in social services and hospitals. Scandals are likely as contracting out escalates and firms fail to provide the required services or refuse to renew contracts. In this situation, the Tories may well develop the idea of an intermediary 'third force', effectively outside the public sector. They did this in the housing sector with housing associations (and their proposals were enthusiastically adopted by the Labour government in 1974). The same arguments were used then about the 'inefficiency', bureaucracy and unresponsiveness of services. A similar type of organisation to housing associations might be set up to take over parts of services. Government policy and funding would then be constructed so as to channel funding and work to these organisations at the expense of public services. After a few years they would be declared 'successful'—exactly what has happened to housing associations. Such schemes would undoubtedly be strongly supported by the SDP and Liberals.

Privatisation isn't a one-off decision. There are also knock-on effects. Contractors will want higher profits and rationalisation through further job cuts. They will also want to expand, either by taking on new areas of work or by extending their operations to adjacent authorities—or both.

As the economic crisis deepens and the financial screw tightens on local government, the pressure for privatisation will increase. The next step after contracting out catering, cleaning and the running of leisure centres, swimming pools, parks, and so on, will be to sell them off entirely to the private sector. While income from such sales might help to ameliorate the immediate financial situation for a council, it will only store up problems for subsequent years.

Government strategy to increase privatisation in other local government services is linked to the Rate Support Grant, or the sum given by central government to supplement local government's income from rates. Each year the government has reduced the percentage of local government spending financed by central government—another cut of 3.1 per cent for 1983–84 brings the level down to 53 per cent. 'Overspending' controls have been tightened and many of the larger urban authorities are likely to make further cuts in services. Preoccupation with the cost of services and tighter central government controls will also push more and more councils to consider privatisation.

The main areas of public spending (after defence and social security/unemployment benefit) are health, education and social services. These services are likely to feel the brunt of the privatisation campaign. They have a high proportion of women workers. The increased emphasis on 'community care' means using free female labour, as far as the Tories are concerned. The use of vouchers has major long-term implications. The state could regulate the value of vouchers, like taxes, increasing personal funding which in turn will lead to further privatisation of services. The sky is virtually the limit for the Tories.

3.

The New Right and the Multinational Offensive

The creation of myths and propaganda has played a key role in the Tories' strategy. Complex issues have been over-simplified into facile slogans. The Tories' attacks on public services and praise for the private sector omit vital evidence, conceal real costs and confuse causes and effects. Yet this propaganda has helped create conditions in which privatisation is tolerated and can flourish. It is also used to divert attention away from the advantages of public services and to try to crush socialist ideas and principles. Propaganda about the advantages of share ownership, your own slice of capitalism, distracts attention from the fundamental issue of *control*. Small shareholders have no control of companies; it is simply an investment. Similarly, home ownership has brought no control of building societies, construction companies, estate agents or changes in the pattern of land ownership. Three per cent of the population still own 74 per cent of the land.

It would be easy to caricature personalities like Thatcher, Joseph, Brittan, Lawson and Fowler as modern-day bandits asset stripping the public sector. But the Tory leadership is supported by an aggressive network of right-wing pressure groups, employers' organisations, financial institutions and multinational companies. Their ideas are fundamental to Conservative Central Office thinking, and have been publicised by the media.

Many aspects of their propaganda campaign are not new. The same organisations have colluded to make similar demands for years. Many of their activities are part of the daily activities of capitalist organisations. What is new is that a right-wing Tory government and an economic recession have created glasshouse conditions for these born-again capitalists to go forth and multiply.

This chapter examines the main myths about privatisation in the light of the real facts. The following chapter describes the different right-wing and business organisations orchestrating the campaign for more privatisation.

Myth 1: privatisation creates a company owning democracy

> *The Public Sector for the Public* (Title of Economic Progress Report, Treasury, May 1982)
>
> The introduction of competion must whenever possible be linked to a transfer of ownership to private citizens and away from the state. Real public ownership—that is ownership by people—must be and is our ultimate goal. (Nicholas Ridley, Financial Secretary to the Treasury, 12 February 1982)

These statements illustrate the Tory tactic of convincing people that privatisation is a means of spreading wealth and ownership, that more and more people are buying shares and benefiting from the capitalist system. The reality is completely different. This doesn't deter the Tories.

Increased share ownership through privatisation is being encouraged in the following ways:

1. *Sale of shares*. Over 600 million shares in BP, British Aerospace, Amersham, Cable and Wireless and Britoil have been offered for sale since the Tories came to power. The proposed sell-off of British Telecom, British Airways and others will bring the total to over one billion.

2. *Management buy-outs of nationalised firms and subsidiaries*. Management, in co-operation with a bank or other financial institutions, buys a percentage of the shares. The remainder are acquired by the financial institutions and other employees. The National Freight Corporation and Victaulic (a profitable British Steel Corporation subsidiary making pipes and fittings) have both been sold in this way. Management buy-outs are in fact more common in the private sector. For instance, in 1981 eight financial groups arranged 124 sales worth £100 million; managers bought between 10 per cent and 85 per cent of the companies.

3. *The establishment of business co-operatives*. There are already about 500 co-ops in Britain, of varying size. Following a major review of the Co-operative Development Agency (CDA) its funds were cut by a third and a new director and board appointed. While local CDAs are being set up to give practical support and advice, the national CDA has adopted a much more market-

orientated approach, presenting co-ops simply as a form of business organisation. 'The Conservative Government wants to see more people having a positive stake in their own business,' is how the Conservative Research Department summed it up in a letter to the Enfield CDA.

Following the sale of British Aerospace, in February 1981, there were 157,829 shareholders in the company, of whom just over 40,000 had under 100 shares. Within a year, the total had plummeted to 27,175, of whom only 3,279 owned under 100 shares. The number of shareholders holding 1 million or more shares had jumped from one to thirteen. The same happened in Cable and Wireless. Nearly 150,000 people acquired shares in October 1981; within two months there were only 27,000 shareholders. Amersham International was sold in February 1982 and 65,000 people acquired shares; by June there were just 8,601 shareholders. Less than 9 per cent of the company's shares are in holdings smaller than £12,000, while nearly two-thirds are concentrated in lots of £250,000 or more.

As soon as shares in these companies were traded on the Stock Exchange their price shot upwards (see Table 1).

Table 1: **Getting rich quick on the Stock Exchange**

	Cost of share	Price at end of first day	Highest price 1982–83
British Aerospace	150p	171p	263p
Cable and Wireless	168p	197p	435p
Amersham International	142p	188p	291p
Britoil	215p	81p*	188p
Associated British Ports	112p	138p	164p

* Based on part-paid shares at 10p

All share offers were oversubscribed—British Aerospace, 2.5 times; Cable and Wireless, 4.6 times; Amersham International, 24.6 times; and Associated British Ports, 34 times. The big decline in the number of shareholders came about because many sold to make a quick financial killing.

To avoid further scandals, the government changed the sale of shares in Britoil to sale by tender instead of a fixed-price offer. Special efforts were made to attract small investors. These included loyalty bonuses of one free share for every ten held for more than three years; simplified application forms obtainable from post offices and banks; payment in two instalments; and the option to buy at the 'striking price' (that at which they were actually sold) rather than having to tender. Just over 255 million shares went on sale on 12 November 1982 at 215p each (£1 payable then and the rest in April 1983) in multiples of 100. Only 27.4 per cent of the offer was taken up, leaving 185.4 million shares in the hands of the financial institutions who had underwritten the offer to guarantee that the government received the full £548 million asking price. At the time of sale, only 9.1 per cent of shareholders owned between 100 and 10,000 shares. When the £1 partly-paid shares started trading on the Stock Exchange they were valued at only 81p at the end of the first day. Small shareholders were discouraged by this and by the doubts raised immediately before the sale, when it was claimed that imminent changes in oil prices would reduce Britoil's future profit levels.

The evidence shows that small investors who could afford to buy shares in British Aerospace, Cable and Wireless and Amersham International soon got rid of them for speculative gains. Small investors have clearly adopted a strategy of 'buy and then sell or don't buy at all' when it comes to share sales from privatisation.

Employee share ownership/profit sharing schemes are now finding favour with the Tories, SDP and Liberals as another means of achieving 'real public ownership'. Employee share ownership schemes were set up with the recent sale of nationalised industries, and involve trustees, often directors of the company, holding shares on behalf of employees. Employees of Cable and Wireless own 0.001 per cent of the company, 0.005 per cent at Amersham and 0.2 per cent at Britoil. And that can hardly be constructed as ownership, let alone control.

So Tory claims about the 'public sector for the public' are fallacious. With 4.5 million people unemployed and wage increases often well below the level of inflation there aren't that many who can spare the odd £200–£4,000 to invest in shares. In reality, the sale of shares in privatised services and industries simply gives the rich the chance to get even richer by gambling on the Stock Exchange.

Share ownership is more and more concentrated in the financial institutions like banks, pension funds, insurance companies and investment trusts. Forty years ago, private individuals owned more than 80 per cent of the ordinary share capital of British companies quoted on the Stock Exchange. That figure is now down to between 28 and 36 per cent. Less than 5 per cent of the population own stocks and shares. The sale of nationalised industries is not going to reverse that trend.

Theoretically, management or worker buy-outs will also lead to a spread in ownership. Collectively, however, workers will only have a tiny percentage share and no real control of the firm through ownership. What they will have, of course, is the illusion of ownership and the illusion of a vested interest in the firm's profitability. This is really what the Tories are after. They hope to create a new breed of worker–capitalists, more concerned with increasing annual dividends by cutting production costs than with the protection of their working conditions.

More free share schemes, loans and other schemes are likely to be developed to entice small investors and employees into ownership. The Treasury is discussing new schemes. In July 1982, the topic was on the agenda of a private conference, held by the Institute of Directors, Aims of Industry and Taylor Woodrow; five members of the Cabinet were present:

> We continue to attach great importance to employees at all levels having the opportunity to build up a capital stake. Our aim is wider ownership. And our housing policy, of course, is equally aimed in that direction. (Sir Geoffrey Howe at the Conservative Political Centre Summer School, Cambridge, 3 July 1982)

The propaganda on share ownership masks the fact that workers' pension funds have massive share and property holdings in Britain and overseas. Together with insurance companies they are the major source of investment capital in Britain. Their combined assets come to over £150 billion. Overseas investment has soared since the Tories lifted exchange controls in 1979, and public sector pension funds now have major stakes in the multinational companies competing for contracts in local government and the NHS. For example, South Yorkshire County Council Pension Fund has shares in Pritchards and Grand Metropolitan. Many of the funds bought shares in British Aerospace, Cable and Wireless, Amersham International and Britoil and are likely to provide the government with substantial finance from future sales of assets like British Telecom. Workers have virtually no control over the funds' investment policies. The Tories are likely to use further claims about 'real public ownership' to head off demands by the trade union movement for greater control over pension fund investment decision.

Myth 2: privatisation increases our freedom

> We want to roll back the frontiers of the state. We need a
> partnership between the public and private sectors. Each
> sector should be able to contribute to the delivery of public
> services what it does best. (Michael Heseltine speaking at
> CBI/Local Government Chronicle Contracting Out Confer-
> ence, 30 November 1982)

The Tories are playing on people's discontent with many publicly
run services. They have pushed through spending cuts and policy
changes designed specifically to intensify dissatisfaction. They are
not attempting to tackle any of the fundamental problems associated with running public services, they are doing absolutely nothing to make services more accountable or to make them more
sensitive to social needs. 'Rolling back the frontiers' simply means
cutting back the role of public sector to allow private firms to gain
a larger slice of work.

Whilst giving the impression that rolling back the state is 'freeing
the citizens from control by the state', the Tories are in fact
changing and increasing centralised power. They have also centralised control over local government spending through the Local
Government Finance Act 1982 and other controls noted in Chapter 2. This again has been dressed up as greater 'freedom'—
freedom to spend less money under tighter controls on a narrower
range of services. For those workers made redundant through
privatisation of services, unemployment means not only a big cut
in living standards but also increased dealings with the state to
obtain benefits.

Meanwhile, the role of the state has expanded in two areas—
defence and the police. Defence spending in 1983–84 is nearly 20
per cent higher in real terms than it was in the first year of Tory
rule. Large wage increases, new equipment and greater powers of
search and arrest have encouraged the expansion of the police
force. This is designed to cope with the increasing level of crime
caused, in part, by mass unemployment, and to counter any
resistance to government policies by the labour movement. Stronger policing means greater state control of picketing, strikes and
occupations.

Such measures are a far cry from a decrease in the role of the
state.

Politicians increasingly advocate the 'mixed economy' approach, claiming that it combines the best of both the public and private sectors. Funnily enough, those who argue in this way usually believe that, ultimately, the public sector is best at doing the unprofitable work.

So, in effect, the state provides a safety net for contractors. For the poor and destitute, the state is the last resort. For contractors, it guarantees profits by ensuring that unprofitable, tedious work is done by the state itself. It is also there to make good the mistakes made by contractors and to take over contracts in the case of bankruptcy.

Of course, this is an untenable position for the public sector, which must be able to run comprehensive services. That means combining the routine with the one-off jobs, the prestigious with the less glamorous work, the profitable with the unprofitable, and so on. This is the way that users will get a good quality *service* at reasonable cost.

Myth 3: privatisation eliminates waste

> [Public services are] expensive, wasteful, inefficient and in-
> adequate. (Michael Forsyth, *Reservicing Britain*, Adam
> Smith Institute, 1981)

The right constantly make such statements about the public sector, at the same time claiming that market forces in the private sector ensure maximum use of resources and fulfilment of consumer needs. Let's look at the reality.

Privatisation has cost millions of pounds—money wasted and spent in a totally non–productive way. The sale of publicly owned land and council houses has lined the pockets of solicitors, sur-veyors and estate agents. In the first three years of Tory rule, over £230 million of public land, owned by New Towns, Property Services Agency and other authorities, was sold. Over 2,500 acres of council housing land and over 400,000 council houses were also sold. Another 160,000 house sales were in the pipeline or expected to be completed in 1982–83. These sales have cost nearly £100 million in fees to solicitors and estate agents. Not one new house was added to the stock, not a sod of turf upturned to develop underused land—yet over 2,500 new council houses could have been built with this money.

The cost of selling shares in BP, British Aerospace, Cable and Wireless, Amersham and Britoil was £42.7 million, most of which went in fees to stockbrokers and merchant banks such as N.M. Rothschild and Sons, Morgan Grenfell and Co., and Phillips and Drew. The sale of £200 million worth of shares in National Enterprise Board companies and other firms cost £3 million in fees alone. Fees to cover the sale of British Telecom will cost another £50 million. In the case of Britoil, stockbrokers', gains from fee income will be offset in the short term by losses incurred in the sale. Stockbrokers and merchant banks underwrote it, which meant they had to retain unsold shares, enabling the government to receive the full value of the sale. However, immediate losses will be offset by future profits from share price rises and by tax dodges. One firm of stockbrokers was reported to be setting up a 'bed and breakfast' deal by selling 10 million Britoil shares, immediately repurchasing them and offsetting the loss against tax charges.

With the exception of Britoil many public assets have been sold at knockdown prices—another form of waste. Figures issued by the Treasury conceal both the costs of sales and their real value by showing only net reductions in expenditure. For example net income from the sale of British Aerospace is shown as £43 million. But this does not take into account £55 million which the government had loaned the corporation. In fact, the real net 'income' is a £12 million deficit. Following an investigation into share sale by the House of Commons Committee of Public Accounts, the Department of Industry reluctantly accepted this figure. If the injection of public money into British Aerospace since 1977 is taken into account, the deficit is £135.4 million. The same goes for Associated British Ports, sold in February 1983. Because the government cancelled three-quarters of its debt, the £22 million sale actually resulted in a net loss of £35 million.

Further waste is evident from the undervaluing of shares in British Aerospace, Cable and Wireless and Amersham International which sold at a substantial premium on the Stock Exchange. Taking their highest share price in 1982, the three sales showed a combined undervaluing of £441 million. Average discounts of 42 per cent on council house sales means the government has given away over £2,000 million to better-off council tenants.

There is also waste from the duplication of services by both public and private sectors. Project Mercury, invested in to the tune of £50 million, doesn't provide any new services or anything which British Telecom cannot provide. In the case of health care, insurance schemes, which are more expensive to run anyway, duplicate the administration of the NHS. Furthermore, up to £90 million will be lost in revenue by the government agreeing to refund VAT paid by health authorities on services provided by private firms.

Individuals and financial institutions who invested in British Aerospace, BP, Cable and Wireless, Amersham International, Britoil and Associated British Ports paid out £1,303 million. When Britain's public services and industry are starving for lack of investment this expenditure produced not one extra job, machine, building or product. Net income was only about half this total after sales costs, government purchase of shares, and the write-off of previous public investment are taken into account. Income from the sale of other companies, land and buildings runs into millions. None of this money has led directly to cuts in taxes, which are higher now than they were in 1979. However, it has been used to keep the level of public spending and the Public Sector Borrowing Requirement slightly lower than they would otherwise have been.

The Tories justify everything in terms of increasing efficiency and abolishing waste. They act as though they have some kind of monopoly on the issue, ignoring the fact that socialists have consistently campaigned against the monumental waste that occurs in the private sector. The efficiency debate is coloured by hypocrisy. We have already looked at the way money is frittered away in sales of shares, council houses and superfluous provision of services that already exist. Margaret Thatcher herself has played job creator when it came to her own office—five new jobs have brought the total to sixty-eight.

Yet the propaganda persists, all the time focusing on the question of efficiency and excluding or undermining the vital issue of the *effectiveness* of services. Report after report recommends ways in which services should be retailored along the lines of successful supermarkets. A business team, led by the managing director of Sainsbury's, carried out an efficiency study in the NHS. Lord Rayner of Marks and Spencer investigated various government departments, the MSC in Northern Ireland, and the NHS. Such reports provide ammunition for cutting labour costs regardless of the consquences measured in human terms. For instance, the Council of Civil Service Unions' response to the government's 1982 White Paper on efficiency and effectiveness in the Civil Service showed that 'cuts have led to loss of effectiveness, lost income, reduced control, and poorer standards of equity'. A number of union case studies in Inland Revenue, Department of Health and Social Security, and the Ministries of Defence and Agriculture, Fisheries and Food highlighted the need simultaneously to assess output and the quality of service if cuts 'achievement' claimed by the government were to be seen as anything other than spurious.

Any attempt to compare efficiency between the public and private sectors is extremely difficult because it is almost impossible to compare like with like. Even comparing costs between public bodies is difficult because of varying policies, needs and geography. But at the very least we can say that there's no hard evidence to support the Tories' case. For example, the massive expansion of housing associations in the early 1970s was based partly on claims that they were more efficient than local authorities. Yet when a House of Commons Committee investigated, neither housing associations nor the Department of the Environment could produce any evidence to prove the claim.

Transferring work to the private sector can be expensive. The hiving-off of Department of Transport road construction design and supervision to fifteen private consultants has increased costs. Redundancy payments and special fees to the consultant cost £5 million. Since it is more expensive to use consultants than Road Construction Units, there will be a continuing extra cost, £4 million in 1981–82 alone. The Department admitted to the House of Commons Public Accounts Committee that they had known in March 1980 that privatisation was going to be more expensive. David Howell, Minister of Transport, claimed the extra costs were outweighed by the advantages to the country of strengthening private consultants. Using private accountants for NHS audits is also more expensive. A DHSS letter to the trade union side admits 'the tenders received were significantly more expensive than the costs of carrying out the work using Civil Service staff'.

Reagan's promise to slash Federal government jobs in the States has had its problems too. The elimination of 43,000 jobs, mainly in domestic programmes, was supposed to save £19 million in 1981 and £838 million the following year. However, the General Accounting Office (GAO) found massive costs had not been accounted for. Redundancy payments, unemployment benefits and early retirement payments cost more than £180 million. The GAO couldn't calculate the loss of productivity, the cost of moving workers to new locations, appeals and grievances. They concluded long-range savings could not be guaranteed. Meanwhile the Defense Department increased its staff by 7.4 per cent.

British Airways' £545 million loss in 1981–82 is another target for the right-wing claims that state enterprises are inefficient and expensive. But BA is a classic example of a state service being 'fitted-up' for sale to the private sector. The 'fitting-up' of BA has involved cutting the workforce of the world's largest international airline from 58,000 in 1979 to 35,000 in 1983, as well as eliminating routes and overseas stations. The entire £199 million redundancy costs were pushed into the 1981–82 accounts. They also included an extraordinary charge of £208 million for increased depreciation of aircraft by writing down the value over 10 instead of 16 years. So with a bit more juggling in the 1982–83 accounts it is hoped to make BA into a saleable product. That still leaves the £1.01 billion long-term debt. It is expected that the government will have to write off at least £750 million before any sale of shares takes place. BA was profitable throughout the 1970s until the current crisis hit most of the world's airlines.

The Tories want competition between the public and private sectors. But the private sector will not compete in many services because it cannot extract any profit from the work, unless of course the state subsidises the work. At the same time the public sector is shackled with controls, responsibilities, prohibited areas of operation and financial constraints which the private sector does not have nor would ever accept. The Tories have tried to create the illusion of fair competition between local authority building departments and private builders. For example DLOs cannot take on work in the private sector or in adjoining areas. This often creates difficulty in maintaining a continuous flow of work and maximum use of equipment. Private builders can bid for any work here or abroad. DLOs must have separate accounting systems for repair and maintenance work, highway maintenance, small new building work and larger new building contracts. Contracts which make a surplus can't subsidise those which do not. DLOs have to do unprofitable work which private builders will not touch. Private builders can cross-subsidise different types of work and use profitable contracts to put in low bids for other work.

DLOs have legal and financial constraints on diversifying into other aspects of construction and building materials, production and supply. In contrast private builders have the freedom to diversify into any aspect of industry. All the major firms are multinational companies with many divisions covering building construction, property development, building materials, and numerous other aspects of industry and commerce.

Competition to the Tories is the holy grail—but it does not automatically lead to better services, increased efficiency or innovation. At best, it may lead to cheaper prices and more choice of service for some—at the expense of others. Competition in the private sector also leads to price fixing, cartels and corruption—all rife in the construction and building materials industry. This leads to higher prices and exploitation of the public sector.

Myth 4: privatisation will revive the economy

The strategy for the public sector cannot be viewed in isolation. In three years of Tory rule, unemployment had reached 4.5 million, if we include hidden unemployment and YOPs as well as those officially counted. Since May 1979 nearly 1.5 million manufacturing jobs have been lost and another one million in other businesses and services. Manufacturing output has slumped. The government's 'no bail-out' policy and high interest rates—they reached a peak of 17 per cent in November 1979—have been used to increase the productivity and competitiveness of industry by forcing weaker firms to go to the wall. As a result, bankruptcies and company liquidations in 1982 were respectively 56 per cent and 115 per cent higher than three years earlier. This creates fear of redundancy, closures and unemployment among both workers and managers. It has led to wage cuts and changes in working practices.

The same shake-out in the public sector requires a different and longer-term strategy. This is why the Tories have intensified the privatisation of public services and nationalised industries. Here the government's stategy has been to cut public spending and to reduce the Public Sector Borrowing Requirement (PSBR), which is basically the difference between what the government spends and what it collects in taxes. The size of the PSBR has become an obsession with successive governments over the last ten years. The Tories are particularly concerned about it because they have abandoned the Keynesian approach, which emphasises regulation of demand, in favour of a monetarist strategy which focuses on the supply of money into the system and its effects on interest rates. In money terms, public sector debt has risen sharply since 1974—

doubling to £110 billion in 1979. But if these figures are rendered in *real* money terms, i.e. taking inflation into account, the PSBR actually declined between 1970 and 1979. However, there is little, if any, connection between the size of the PSBR and economic performance. In 1980 only two EEC countries had smaller PSBRs as a proportion of GDP than Britain. Japan's was over 8 per cent—over 2 percentage points higher than Britain's.

The Tories believe that a high PSBR leads to high interest rates which can in turn lead to less investment in the private sector because investors can get a better and/or more secure return for their money by loaning it to the government and public bodies. This is not true. Even when interest rates have fallen, capital expenditure by manufacturing industry has continued to decline—by mid-1982 it was 25 per cent below its 1979 level. Meanwhile, investment overseas has mushroomed since exchange controls were lifted in 1979. The outflow of capital rose to £10.7 billion in 1981 compared with £2.3 million in 1977. Half of this total was direct investment in factories and plants overseas. Most of the rest was accounted for by pension funds and insurance companies investing in stocks and shares in overseas markets and in property abroad. In Britain over £1.6 billion was diverted into the privatisation of state-owned companies—money spent simply to change ownership and not to provide new factories, better services equipment or new jobs.

The PSBR reached a record £13.5 billion in 1980–81, equivalent to 5.9 per cent of the Gross Domestic Product (GDP). The PSBR for 1982–83 is estimated to be £9 billion, falling to £8 billion in 1983–84 (2.75 per cent of GDP). The Tories argue that the PSBR is far too high and that the sale of state assets will help to reduce it. Transferring nationalised industries to the private sector means that all their spending and income is excluded from public accounts. So are loans to help finance new investment. In addition, the government receives income from the sale of assets which it wouldn't otherwise have, hence increasing total income and reducing the amount it needs to borrow at least in the short term. Some right-wing economists disagree with the government's line of reasoning over the PSBR and privatisation. A study into the PSBR commissioned by the right-wing Centre for Policy Studies concluded that

> whilst selling off parts of the nationalised undertakings would
> be consistent with the objective of a smaller public sector it is

unlikely that it would have a major impact upon the total
PSBR over the long run.

The sale of assets contributes to the government's income for
one year only. It also means a loss of income in future years in
dividends from profitable companies. Britoil's 1982 pre-tax profits
are expected to be £473 million. Cable and Wireless's half-yearly
pre-tax profits to September 1982 increased by nearly 50 per cent
to £67 million. Amersham International jumped 38-per cent over
the same period. The Tories, of course, would claim these as
success stories: increased efficiency naturally follows when companies are 'free of the shackles of the state'. But the truth is that
increased profits were helped by lower interest rates and Cable
and Wireless selling 60 per cent and 20 per cent stakes in its
Bahrain and Hong Kong operations. Cable and Wireless shares
rose to 350p. They were originally sold off by the government for
168p, less than half price.

Net income from the actual and planned special asset sales by
central government are as given in Table 2.

Table 2: **Net income from actual and planned special asset sales**

	Net income	Per cent of government's expenditure plans
1979–80	£370m	0.47
1980–81	£405m	0.51
1981–82	£481m	0.46
1982–83	£600m estimate	0.5
1983–84	£750m estimate	0.6

The table shows that income from special sales by central government has, to date, not exceeded 10 per cent of the PSBR.
However, the planned £4 billion sale of British Telecom in
1984–85 could represent about 50 per cent of the PSBR for that
year. But taken has a percentage of total annual government
expenditure, sales income represents less than 1 per cent. The
Telecom sale will bring this up to about 3 per cent. Clearly, the
financial gains from asset sales are not as important to public
spending as the government tries to pretend.

The main financial impact of privatisation has actually been at
local rather than national government level. Council house sales in
most local authorities have been extensive. In three years of Tory
rule, 311,000 council houses were sold in England and Wales with

a capital value of £2,987 million net of discounts. Actual income received from sales was less because when purchasers acquire a council mortgage there is only a paper transaction within the council and income is spread over a number of years.

The government have slashed spending on council housebuilding and now make it dependent on councils' success in selling houses. Already council housebuilding is back to its 1920s level. Only £3,244 million was allocated for capital projects by local authority, new town and housing associations in 1983–84; one-third of this will come from house and land sales. Clearly, council house sales have had a substantial political and economic impact. This has been at the expense of council housebuilding, improvement and repair.

Myth 5: privatisation saves money

Contracting out services has a wider effect on the economy than the claims of 'savings' would suggest. Privatisation often simply shifts the cost on to another budget or authority. For example, the combined annual 'savings' claimed by contracting out refuse collection in Wandsworth, Tandridge and refuse and cleansing in Merton is £446,000. But 185 jobs were lost. Assuming that nearly all these employees did not find other work, this must have cost the state £1 million in the first year alone. (This figure is based on loss of income and indirect taxes, and the paying of unemployment and family income benefits, rent and rate rebates and other benefits for a person earning £6,000, married with two children.) Direct labour proposals to retain the work in the three authorities still meant the loss of 88 jobs. Assuming that these workers remained unemployed, the cost to the state would be £492,000—still more than the 'savings' claimed.

Other economic effects include increased imports and an outflow of profits. For example, British Telecom has an annual investment programme of £2,200 million. Up to now, 95 per cent of BT's purchases have been from companies manufacturing in the UK and employing 70,000 workers. When the government relaxed controls—liberalisation, as it is called—and allowed second phones to be supplied and maintained privately, only 2 out of 96 types of phones submitted for government appoval were made in the UK. Markets for second phones and business telecoms equipment are likely to face massive competition from imports, leading to further loss of jobs in Britain.

Privatisation of major companies and industries leads to the government having even less power to influence investment in key sectors of the economy. Foreign-based multinationals operating private hospitals in Britain are likely to transfer profits overseas. The same goes for oil giants like Exxon (the world's largest corporation) and Conoco (part of the Dupont group), who will probably compete with British Gas to supply industrial users.

The right's vision

Many of these myths derive from the theories of right-wing economists such as Milton Friedman and Friedrich von Hayek. They believe that the market is the best means of allocating and using resources, so long as it is virtually free from state controls and intervention. Friedman constantly harks back to 'the good old days' of British and American capitalism in the mid-nineteenth century. *Free to Choose* by Friedman and Rose explains these ideas and theories and should be read by anyone wanting a deeper insight into ideas and propaganda being pumped out by British devotees such as Margaret Thatcher and Sir Keith Joseph.

Friedman believes the state has only four main functions: defence; administration of justice; the maintenance of certain public services 'unattractive' (i.e. unprofitable) to the private sector; and the protection of those 'who cannot be regarded as "responsible individuals".' He states that welfare services 'weaken the family; reduce the incentive to work, save, and innovate; reduce the accumulation of capital; and limit our freedom'. They also 'poison the springs of private charitable activity'.

Friedman's prescriptions include making individuals responsible for their own pensions by scrapping the state pension scheme, and changing social security to a system of cash income supplements with private charity taking care of those in greater need. He also advocates privatising the NHS. Market competition would rear its ugly head in education too. In Friedman's Utopia, schools would operate on the basis of a voucher system and, in higher education, students would receive loans, not grants. These loans could be from private investors who would 'buy a share in an individual's earning prospects, to advance him (sic) the funds needed to finance his training on condition that he agree to pay the investor a specified fraction of his future earning'. You've heard of equity finance for home ownership, now we bring you equity finance for education ownership, health ownership, and a new guaranteed equity bond for the right to live!

Reading Friedman really clarifies the somewhat murky depths of Thatcherite ideology. Lesser mortals may be confused, but Friedman explains all: 'sincerity is a much overrated virtue'; 'a free market system distributes the fruits of economic progress among all the people'; 'when you vote daily in the supermarket, you get precisely what you voted for, and so does everyone else.' Life is, like a game of cards, a game of chance.

> By the end of the evening, some will be big winners, others big losers. In the name of the ideal of equality, should the winners be required to repay the losers? That would take all the fun out of the game. Not even the losers would like that.

That's what Thatcher means when she says, 'We are all unequal. We believe that everyone has the right to be unequal.'

4.

Who is Behind Privatisation?

Having examined the right's propaganda and myths in the previous chapter, this one investigates their network of organisations and campaigns. These fall into four groups: the Conservative Party and other political parties; right-wing pressure groups; the Confederation of British Industry (CBI) and other employers' organisations; and companies, consultants and financial institutions. They have a common strategy which includes publishing reports on examples of privatisation taken from Britain, USA, Europe and other countries. They usually ignore all the problems associated with private provision, such as the appalling suffering and high costs of health care in the USA or the experience of those who can't afford full or even partial insurance. Companies which have won contracts in Britain have also widely distributed glossy brochures to politicians and officials claiming improved efficiency and big financial savings. Anti-trade union propaganda is pumped out in much the same way. These organisations hold meetings and conferences bringing politicians, officials, and contractors together to discuss the advantages and methods of privatisation. Another strategy involves contractors and consultants carrying out feasibility studies to 'prove' the advantages of privatisation.

The network of links between the organisations, companies and individuals is extensive. The same bankers and stockbrokers who advise the government on the sale of state assets advise companies and the pension funds on investment strategy. Consultants work for the multinational firms whilst advising local authorities on reorganisation and 'efficiency'. Individuals are often active in several organisations and meet together at their clubs and conferences. MPs and government officials are well represented. Big business provides the funding for most of these organisations.

Party lines

Conservative Party Central Office published a *Privatisation Directory* just before the May 1982 local government elections, listing all the services which local authorities had already privatised. This was followed by *Down with the Rates* by Michael Forsyth, a Westminster councillor and consultant to Pritchard Services Group. The Tory Party Conference saw the launch of a draft manifesto by the right-wing Selsdon Group. *A Long Way to Go* called for total denationalisation, the privatisation of nearly all local government services, and the introduction of private health insurance and education voucher schemes.

The Liberals and the Social Democratic Party have been less dogmatic than the Tories, but still advocate a greater role for the private sector in public services. Liberal-controlled Liverpool Council sold council houses and land on a huge scale even before the 1980 Housing Act, ran down the building department and are now seeking ways of privatising refuse collection, cleansing and council housing management. The SDP policy for nationalised industries is 'to expose them to greater competitive forces whenever possible'. Nationalised industries already operating in competition with the private sector would be restructured as private companies, and would gradually pass from public to private ownership through share sales. So you pays your money and takes your choice—foxtrot with the SDP, or tango with the Tories.

Far right pressure groups

Right-wing pressure groups are usually run by academic and business economists and have a long history of organising and supporting right-wing causes. They are well funded and each year spend at least £5 million. The Economic League, founded in 1919, has over 100 staff. Its services to employers include vetting prospective employees for trade union activities. Several organisations have increasingly stronger links with extreme right-wing, pro-nuclear, fundamentalist Christian organisations in the USA: the Heritage Foundation, Moral Majority, and the Committee for the Survival of a Free Congress are some examples.

The Adam Smith Institute (ASI), based in London and Washington, DC, is run by an all-star cast. Friedrich von Hayek, leading monetarist economist, is its chairperson; its executive secretary is Stuart Butler, author of several reports for Aims of Industry including *The American Telephone System: A Blueprint for Denationalisation*. ASI has played a leading role in distributing propaganda about privatisation to councillors, civil servants, and the media. It has published a number of pamphlets—*Reservicing Britain*, *Reservicing Health*, *Economy and Local Government*, and *Working with Contractors*. One, *Private Road Ahead*, calls for companies to build new roads using private finance. Return on investment would come from annual fees paid by the government or from direct charges to users in the form of tolls or automatic metering. The ASI also produced a report, *Privatising Pensions*, which argues for the complete privatisation of state pensions in Britain, along similar lines to Chile.

The ASI also organises right-wing talk-ins. Dr E. S. Savas, one of Reagan's White House aides and a privatisation fanatic, has spoken at these conferences of 'massive savings' to be made.

The Institute for Economic Affairs (IEA) is a research and educational body which specialises in the study of markets and pricing systems. Not surprisingly, it has called for the introduction of insurance schemes, vouchers and voluntary labour in education, health and other services. A recent publication, *The Welfare State: For Rich or for Poor?* argued for a resurrection of the nineteenth-century system of 'mutual aid', under which health and housing are dependent on charity and friendly societies. Arthur Seldon, in another IEA offering called *Wither the Welfare State*, claimed that 'When the Social Democrats understand the army they will lead, they could go further than the Conservatives in loosening state welfare'. He also discussed 'liquidating the welfare state as an act of patriotism'.

The director of the IEA is Lord Harris of High Cross, whose book *The Challenge of a Radical Reactionary* was published by the Centre for Policy Studies (CPS). CPS was set up in 1974 by Sir Keith Joseph and Margaret Thatcher to provide them and other right-wing Tories with monetarist policies and propaganda. It has published various pamphlets and books including *The New Conservatism* by Nigel Lawson, Financial Secretary to the Treasury, and *The Right to Learn*. The latter attacks comprehensive education and includes an article on education vouchers by Marjorie Seldon, wife of free marketeer and IEA journal editor Arthur Seldon. Other recent CPS publications include *Telecommunications in Britain: Switching Direction* and *The Truth about Trans-*

port. The former, undertaken at the prompting of the Department of Industry, examines the implications of the British Telecommunications Act 1981 and the future of British Telecom. It concludes that

> if telephone services to rural areas or special groups such as OAPs are thought to be a social necessity, then they should be funded by local authorities, Development Boards or social agencies, not by a commercial company.

An ex-director of CPS is David Young, previously 'industrial adviser' to Sir Keith Joseph and now chairperson of the Manpower Services Commission. The government is currently examining ways of hiving-off parts of the employment service.

There are more insidious organisations clamouring for privatisation. Aims of Industry has attacked local authority Direct Labour Organisations consistently over the last few years, and the Freedom Association, well known for its hostility to many trade union activities, particularly at Grunwicks, regularly praises the work of contractors in its newspaper *The Free Nation*. Aims of Industry plans a £1 million campaign against the Labour Party's nationalisation proposals. Its vice-president is Sir Frank Taylor of builders Taylor Woodrow. Recently given a peerage by Margaret Thatcher, he is also on the Freedom Association's governing council.

Others, such as the Argonauts, operate more secretly. The Argonauts are a 'club' of Thatcher's staunchest business allies. Meeting regularly, their principal aim seems to be to ensure that the Tories maintain a hard line against trade unions. But they are also keen on privatisation of the nationalised industries. The group includes Alfred Sherman, who is head of the Centre for Policy Studies, and leader writer of the *Daily Telegraph*. The *Observer* noted that his 'enthusiasm for capitalism is akin to the zeal of a reborn Christian'. Another Argonaut is Thatcher's chief economic adviser, Professor Alan Walter, vice-president of the Selsdon Group. The Centre for Policy Studies pays £12,500 towards his salary. Michael Ivens, director of Aims of Industry, and Walter Goldsmith, director general of the Institute of Directors, are both Argonauts. So are representatives of other business organisations such as the National Federation of Building Trades Employers, Engineering Employers' Federation and the Association of British Chambers of Commerce.

Employers' organisations

The Confederation of British Industry has called for legislation comparable to controls on DLOs to apply to all public services, but with much lower tendering limits. It has also called for consumer charges to be applied to more services; the introduction of contractors to run the fire services, halls of residence and catering at universities and colleges; and the sale of further state assets. The CBI's views were summed up by its Director General, Sir Terence Beckett: 'If the whole country were made an enterprise zone and removed from the crippling burden of business rates and planning restrictions then we might really be talking.'

The National Federation of Building Trades Employers (NFBTE) and the Federation of Master Builders (FMB) lobbied long and hard to get the Tory government to impose controls on DLOs and create more work for private builders. The NFBTE has been monitoring local authorities' contracts awarded to DLOs in order to make the government tighten controls still further.

Walter Goldsmith, Director General of the Institute of Directors, recently called for contractors to have a statutory right to tender for local government services. He re-emphasised the Institute's commitment to greater privatisation and advocated businesspeople's involvement in deciding local authority spending plans. He has also called for the government not only to give loss-making nationalised industries to the private sector, but also to pay the private sector to 'remove the burden'.

As far as Goldsmith is concerned

> the crucial issue is public sector monopoly unionism. It is industrial action in the public sector which presents the gravest threat for the immediate future. If nothing is done to contain the bargaining power of public sector unions, they will be able to undermine the effectiveness of all the employment legislation so far introduced by the present government, and obtain excessive wage increases. If this occurs it will not be long before unions operating in the private sector follow suit. The priority for action must therefore be to break the bargaining monopolies in the public sector.

And the best means of achieving this? 'A massive programme of privatisation'.

Companies and consultants

The privatisation of public services opens up a multi-billion pound market for financial institutions, such as banks, building societies, insurance companies, pension funds and industrial and commercial companies.

Multinational companies will benefit more than local firms. They have the financial resources to put in leader tenders at a loss in order to get a foot in the door—in the anticipation of profitable contracts later. They also have various divisions covering many different industries, products and services, which means they can buy or transfer products within the company at a lower cost than purchasing from other companies. Multinationals can consequently use the technique of 'transfer pricing' by inflating or deflating the prices paid between subsidiaries and individual plants to suit the company's overall needs. Their resources enable them to move around the world opening and closing plants, introducing new machinery and technology and seeking new contracts, with relative ease but with dire results for workers. They have the power to take over smaller firms in their search for diversification or a larger share of the market. For example, Brengreen (Exclusive Cleaners), which has several local authority contracts for refuse collection, could easily be gobbled up by Grand Metropolitan. Companies taken over are then rationalised and reorganised, usually with job losses. In addition, multinationals have a great deal of political power, which enables them to influence different governments' economic and industrial policies, both here and overseas. Their links with the City are strong: insurance companies, pension funds and banks invest heavily in them and provide loan finance for new ventures.

Privatisation is encouraging even stronger alliances between financial institutions and companies. Project Mercury is financed by Cable and Wireless, BP and Barclays Bank. Barclays is also involved with Abbey National Building Society and Barratts, Britain's largest private housebuilder, in the privatisation of a large council estate in Knowsley (see page 11). Sir Laurie Barratt, speaking at a Stock Exchange conference in 1982, stated that: 'Another new segment of the market we have analysed is the renovation, instead of the demolition, of the unfit local authority houses.' Barratts have already made bargain puchases of 300 dwellings from Liverpool council. Aided by improvement grants from the council, Barratts will revamp the properties before selling them off.

> Such is our conviction that this vast number of local authority houses can be saved up and down the country and sold to the private sector that we are in the process of setting up four new subsidiaries to do nothing else but specialise in this field.

Multinationals well-versed in modern American union-busting techniques—for example the Hospital Corporation of America—are the same companies now operating in Britain and exploiting the privatisation of public services. AFL–CIO's assistant organising director, Charles McDonald, summed up their tactics:

> I think it's sophisticated and controlled terrorism. What they do in an organising compaign is nothing short of a terrorist campaign, working as much as they can to exploit the fears that employees have of losing their job.

Union-busting consultants from the USA (for example, Modern Management Methods) now have offices in Britain. Conferences and courses on union busting are being held in Britain. Their aim is not to get controllable, pliable unions or staff associations, but to abolish them altogether.

Below is a brief profile of three companies who are gaining substantially from privatisation.

Pritchard Services Group

Pritchard has various divisions and subsidiary companies, covering office and factory cleaning (Cleaners Ltd and General Cleaning Contractors Ltd); refuse collection and street cleaning (Pritchard Industrial Services Ltd); linen and workwear rental (United Linen); stone cleaning and preservation (London Stone Ltd); hospital healthcare services (Crothall and Co. Ltd); and security guards (Pritchards Security Services Ltd).

It has 74 subsidiary companies in 20 countries overseas, including South Africa (4), the USA (5), Australia (6), and New Zealand (10). A major recent takeover was the US-based National Medical Consultants (£45 million sales in 1981), which has been merged with Crothalls to form the second largest hospital services firm in North America, supplying cleaning, laundry, engineering and maintenance services to over 225 hospitals.

Recent British contracts include street cleansing in Wandsworth, cash security services for Kingston-upon-Thames, cleaning of 90 per cent of London's Underground stations and cleaning services at the 280-bed Princess Alexandra Hospital, Swindon.

Pritchard's have lately won further large hospital contracts in Kuwait and have linked up with the American firm Waste Management Inc to win £395 million contracts to clean the Saudi Arabian cities of Jeddah and Riyadh. Turnover has grown from £27 million in 1973 to over £273 million in 1982. Profits increased by 67 per cent in 1982; overseas profits trebled.

Grand Metropolitan Ltd
One of Britain's major multinational companies, with turnover reaching £3,849 million in 1982 with pre-tax profits of £220 million, a 45 per cent rise in the last two years. Grandmet recently took over refuse collection in Chelsea and street cleaning in Wandsworth; it has done studies on school meals reorganisation for Oxfordshire County Council, and is reportedly interested in taking over council house management in Liverpool.

Grandmet owns Watney Mann and Truman Breweries, Express Dairy (including Ski yoghurts, and Eden Vale products), Berni Inns, and over 60 hotels. The recent takeover of Intercontinental Hotel Corporation from PanAm has added a further 100 hotels in the USA and elsewhere. It also owns Mecca Leisure and 620 betting shops, Warner Holidays, International Distillers (J & B Scotch Whisky, Gilbey's Gin, Croft Port, etc.). Grandmet Services for Hospitals provides catering, housekeeping and maintenance services to 60 British hospitals, manages one and is building another. Grandmet Catering Services runs 1,500 industrial restaurants, making it the second largest catering contractor in Britain.

Grandmet employs over 100,000 workers in Britain (one-third are part-time) and nearly 30,000 overseas. In 1982 two directors each received more than £250,000 in salaries (excluding pensions contributions).

Hospital Corporation of America (HCA)
Now the world's largest private health company, it owns or manages 362 hospitals—or 51,000 beds—in the USA, Australia, India, Saudi Arabia and Latin America. It also runs 25 psychiatric hospitals in the USA. In Brazil, HCA's Health Maintenance Organisation provides 'total health care'—hospitals, clinics and physicians—for 640,000 people, the largest contract of its type outside the USA. Turnover in 1982 was expected to reach £2,400 million, and the company expects this to double every three years. It currently has an operating profit margin of 14 per cent. Last year HCA bought Hospital Affiliates International (HAI) from the

Insurance Company of North America for over £300 million. HAI owned the 120-bed Cromwell Hospital in West London. HCA itself is currently trying to develop private hospitals in Southampton and Edinburgh. It has a range of subsidiary companies involved in health care, leasing and insurance. Prudential Insurance owns 6 per cent of the shares. HCA recently announced that it had paid £14 million to acquire a majority interest in six private hospitals owned by Seltahart Holdings and Y. J. Lovell Holdings, the construction and property group.

American multinationals are profiteering in telecommunications as well as in health care. Following deregulation in the USA, both American Telephone and Telegraph and Western Union have set up bases in Britain to compete with British Telecom in supplying technology which would enable electronic office machines to be plugged into international telecommunications networks. It is precisely this area which is at the forefront of British Telecom's survival strategy.

Internationally, privatisation mania has been good news for big business. The Pinochet regime in Chile has recently invited British companies to participate in the running of public utility services on a commercial basis. Any company wanting to build a power station in Chile will be allowed to sell electricity on the national grid. Privatisation of water supplies to Chilean cities is also on offer. In 1981 the London-registered Autofagasta and Bolivia Railway Company distributed nearly 4 million cubic metres of water in northern Chile.

Working hand in glove with the multinationals are management consultants such as Coopers and Lybrand, Price Waterhouse, and Peat, Marwick and Mitchell. They are gaining substantial contracts for reorganisation and efficiency studies, which often lead to privatisation. Claims of impartiality for their studies ring hollow since these firms are also accountants for many of the multinational companies. For example, Peat, Marwick and Mitchell audit British Aerospace, British Steel Pension Fund, Tarmac, Costain and Town and City Properties. They are also advisers to the London Docklands Development Board. One of their senior partners was a member of the Serpell Inquiry into British Rail's finances. Coincidentally, Peat, Marwick and Mitchell received over £100,000 in consultancy fees from the inquiry.

Price Waterhouse are accountants for Barclays Bank, Chase

Manhattan Bank, Reckitt and Coleman, Legal and General Insurance, Eagle Star Insurance and Land Securities, Britain's largest property company. They also produced the British Airways reorganisation report and recently extended their audit of Birmingham Council's accounts to include an efficiency study in the social services department. Price Waterhouse have a Local Government Services Department. Their publicity material describes its work:

> Replace the profit motive which is normally present in commercial organisations by the demand to provide a service to the public at an economic cost and the two are not that dissimilar. Thus, a major feature of our service to the public sector has been the development of sophisticated money and efficiency review techniques.

Coopers and Lybrand is the world's largest management consultancy firm, followed by Peat, Marwick and Mitchell; both are American. The latter, which has 300 offices in 80 countries, had a worldwide fee income of £675 million in 1982.

Financial institutions are also involved in pursuing the privatisation of public housing and land particularly in inner-city areas. Following the 1981 riots in Toxteth, Liverpool, the Financial Institution Group (FIG) was set up by Michael Heseltine, then Secretary of State for the Environment. Twenty-six of its members were seconded from banks, city institutions and private companies. The function of FIG is to examine inner-city problems and to identify opportunities for private sector finance. It initiated the £70m Urban Development and Action Grant, modelled on American attempts to use public money to support 'marginal' private initiatives and turn them into profitable schemes. It has also examined schemes for privatising council house management by handing over groups of 5,000 council houses to tenants or private management companies for 'intensive management'. This scheme was evidently shelved because of the political repercussions, but FIG is going ahead with plans to privatise empty council houses.

FIG has developed a scheme to channel money from pension funds to expand owner occupation via private builders and housing associations. Organisations such as the United Kingdon Housing Trust have developed similar proposals, linking up pension fund money with building societies for private housebuilding or the expansion of private renting. This will effectively privatise the design, building, management and repair of housing.

Britain's multinational insurance companies see a large potential market for health, education, personal insurance and pensions. Although private health insurance is currently run mainly by BUPA and two smaller insurance organisations, future expansion is likely to be captured by the major companies. The major insurance companies already invest about 20 per cent of their funds in property development and there is no reason to suppose they'll pass up the rich pickings to be had from privatisation of other services.

5.

The Effects of Privatisation on Workers, Users and Services

Privatisation has wide-ranging implications.

First, there will be a dramatic change in the composition of the labour market as large numbers of public employees move into the private sector. Given the differing levels of pay, benefits, conditions, and trade union organisation, the impact is likely to be significant.

Second, it will have a profound effect on women's employment. Although the privatisation of refuse collection, building repair, etc., hits male manual workers, other services currently being privatised or under threat employ mostly female labour. This will accelerate the already rapid rise in unemployment: since 1976, unemployment among women has increased at twice the male rate. Privatisation also increases pressure on women to do the same work, such as childcare and caring for the sick and elderly—but unpaid and in the isolation of their own homes.

Third, privatisation can speed up the process of mechanisation and introduction of new technology. Shedding labour, scrapping existing working arrangements, getting rid of workplace trade union organisation, and loosening political control create, as far as the Tories and their allies are concerned, an opportunity to introduce machines and new technology without agreement.

Fourth, privatisation has long-term financial effects on individuals and the state. Far from achieving savings and 'cuts in the rates burden', the sale of assets and services will lead to increased government spending to cover increased supervision, contractors' inferior work and failures, cost overruns, resources wasted by the duplication of 'competitive' services, and the storing-up of problems requiring further expenditure later.

Compulsory redundancies, fewer jobs, worse conditions

It is not just British industry which is shedding jobs. The state is also doing so. Both the threat of privatisation and its actual implementation cause permanent loss of jobs. When it is used as a threat, it leads to public sector workers negotiating to take on more work with fewer workers. Deals are often clinched by management offering a higher bonus in return for workers accepting some redundancies and changes in working arrangements.

The preparation of British Airways for sale has led to 16,000 jobs disappearing in two years, at a cost of £230 million in redundancy payments. The privatisation of British Telecom is speeding up the introduction of new technology—the Post Office Engineering Union estimates that 60,000 jobs will go in the next decade. In British Telecom's factories, 3,700 jobs are threatened because the ending of BT's monopoly has meant that private firms (mainly abroad) are increasingly supplying and maintaining equipment. By the middle of 1982, over 33,000 Civil Service jobs had been lost or were immediately threatened by privatisation in the Property Services Agency, Ministry of Defence and other departments. In January 1983, the Treasury produced another privatisation plan. The *Review of Civil Service Manpower After 1984* showed that up to 60,000 more jobs would be lost. Cleaning, building and ground maintenance, typing, training, catering, security and vehicle maintenance are the services likely to be contracted out.

The privatisation of local authority services has also resulted in about one-third of the jobs affected being permanently lost. Staffing levels in Wandsworth, Southend, Eastbourne and Merton refuse services were slashed when contractors took over. This doesn't mean there was 'fat' to be cut, but indicates how contractors intensify workloads, to the detriment of workers' health and the quality of services. The scale of job losses could be enormous. For example, if contractors manage to gain 20 per cent of the NHS catering and ancillary work, about 40,000 full-time jobs will be lost. While some of these public sector jobs would be replaced by jobs with contractors, many would be permanently lost. Privatisation means unemployment.

The only way contractors can win public sector work is by undercutting wages and benefits and demanding much higher levels of productivity. Employing fewer workers and making them work harder for longer hours reduces costs. They can also sometimes undercut public sector overheads. Wages and conditions in refuse collection and cleansing contractors—Exclusive Cleaners, Pritchard's, Grandmet and Taskmasters (a subsidiary of Alfred Marks)—highlight the differences. Contractors' basic wages were about the same as those in local government. However, working for a contractor meant a longer working week—up to 3½ hours longer, with no 'task and finish'. Under task and finish, workers complete their round and then go home. It originated with consolidating rest allowances allocated to refuse workers because of the heavy nature of the work. Contractors often demanded mandatory Saturday and Sunday working, at normal rate of pay, after every bank holiday weekend. Overtime was usually paid at time-and-a-third instead of time-and-a-half, and there was less opportunity to earn it.

Sickness, pension and holiday entitlements were far inferior working for a contractor. If you became ill, contractors would pay only two to four weeks at full basic pay, then a similar period of half pay. This compared with up to 26 weeks at full pay and 26 at half pay, after seven years' service, in local government. Contractors gave one week's holiday less each year. Pension schemes were also inferior—Pritchard's workers in Wandsworth don't even have one—with pensions based on one-eightieth of wages, compared with three-eightieths in local government.

Many governmental departments, including the Treasury, Ministry of Defence and DHSS, are now cleaned by private contractors. They have undercut Civil Service cleaners by a number of manoeuvres which have nothing to do with efficiency. These include undercutting the set minimum rates of pay—at least 9 per cent of cleaners on government contracts are paid less than this minimum; not paying the normal 5.5 per cent Civil Service allowance for night work; not providing a pension scheme, which Civil Service cleaners get; and working for shorter hours to avoid payment of National Insurance contributions, which saves firms 13.7 per cent of the wages bill. Since 90 per cent of cleaners work less than 16 hours per week, they are not covered by the Employment Protection (Consolidation) Act 1978—so there can be no claims of unfair dismissal.

A 1980 investigation by ACAS into the contract cleaning industry concluded that

A large proportion of general contract cleaners are today among the lowest paid manual workers and the earnings of many fall below standards that have been determined as statutory minima for major groups of unskilled manual workers in wages councils.

Working harder for longer hours leads to more accidents and illness, particularly for those involved in heavy manual work. A revised productivity deal in the refuse section of Newport Pagnell led to an increase in illness. In the first 18 months, two men died, two had back injuries and four couldn't do any heavy work anymore—out of a workforce of twenty-five. These illnesses may not be totally attributable to the increased workload, but it was a contributing factor. In Merton, a revised scheme by the unions meant a 17 per cent increase in workload for refuse workers; the contract was eventually won by Taskmasters, who planned to use 25 per cent fewer workers than the unions' scheme.

Accidents also increase. Contractors constantly try to avoid health and safety provisions. The Health and Safety Executive has shown that accident frequency rates in the private building industry are up to twice those of local authority Direct Labour Organisations. Increased stress at work, and consequently at home, will also take its toll.

Privatisation is an attack on basic trade union organisation. Only 17 per cent of private services are unionised, compared to 52 per cent of the total workforce and much higher levels in the public services. Contractors don't want to know about unions and union activists are rarely re-employed by them. Lack of trade union organisation means that contractors can hire and fire. Just one month after Pritchard's recruited workers in Wandsworth, they started sacking them. Three workers were sacked instantly in March 1982 when they were found to have taken an extra 15 minutes' tea break.

Privatising women's lives and work

The Tories sanctify 'the family' because they want to increase its role as an economic unit to carry out the reproduction of labour. The welfare state and local government services now do some of the work previously carried out almost entirely within the family by women. In dismantling and privatising the welfare state and public services not all the work can be moulded into contracts or transformed into profitable propositions for the private sector. People simply can't afford to pay the high costs of private nurseries and health care. Much of it therefore has to be hived-off to individuals and families.

Propaganda about the family also has its ideological functions. The Tories' aim is to get rid of the idea that taking care of under-fives, the sick and the elderly should even be considered a public responsibility. Privatisation makes it *your* problem. Taking women out of employment reinforces the myth that men are the main breadwinners and that their jobs should be safeguarded whenever possible. In fact, the proportion of women and men who have responsibility for dependent children is almost the same, 38 per cent and 40 per cent respectively.

Cutting back nurseries, the NHS, and social services forces us to take care of the young, the sick and elderly at home. 'Care in the community must mean care by the community,' stated Patrick Jenkin when he was Secretary of State for Health. Yet the Association of Carers reports that many women looking after dependent relatives at home are already being stretched to breaking point.

As well as this increase in unpaid labour in the home, women also face an increase in unpaid work in their jobs. Many school meal workers now find themselves working unpaid extra hours in order to complete their work. Some county councils have shortened working hours, others have abolished school meals, while some, like Kent, have forced women into casual labour by breaking national agreements to pay holiday retaining fees.

Deteriorating services

The British Telecom network has been built up to provide a national integrated service in urban and rural areas for both residential and business users. Privatisation means that operating policies and investment decisions will be made in accordance with BT's marketing strategy for over 60 'profit centres'. Profits and the return on investment will be the determining factors, not services. Charges for services in rural areas, calls from public call boxes, residential off-peak call charges and connection charges for new subscribers are all likely to rise substantially. It is also likely that the benefits of new technology will be concentrated into the most heavily used areas. Of BT's total income, 60 per cent comes from its four million business users (300 companies contribute half of this), the remainder from 15 million residential users. International telephone and telex use represents only 2.1 per cent of traffic, but contributed 48 per cent of profits in 1981–82. So it is easy to see where BT's priorities will lie after privatisation.

The collapse of telephone services for most individual users is likely to be only one of the more minor inconveniences which privatisation will bring. It is worth looking at the likely developments in local government services in this light.

Falling standards. The quality of local government services suffers as a consequence of privatisation. Pritchard Services Group took over street cleansing in Wandsworth in February 1982. At the end of March, the council introduced a penalty system based on inspections of the quality of the work. In a seven-week period (excluding a two-month settling-down period and 10 weeks during which the penalty system was suspended because of the refuse strike), Pritchard's received 1,894 penalty notices, costing them £7,665 in fines. This included 191 major warning notices—yet their contract stated that 25 such notices in any four-week period would render the contract invalid. The council reported that 12 per cent of the streets (about 190 roads) were being swept inadequately or not at all each week—four times the level permitted by the contract. Eastbourne prides itself as the cleanest town in Britain. Exclusive Cleaners won the refuse and street cleaning contract in early 1982. In the summer, the town's image took a bit of a battering as its streets became ever more littered. The council had to increase the number of inspectors, who were working overtime at weekends, to check the quality of the work. Exclusive had to bring in vehicles and crews from its Southend operations in the evenings to keep up with the work. The privatisation of refuse collection also results in much higher charges for trade and garden refuse. In Southend and Eastbourne, charges doubled.

Defects and delays. Women bear the brunt of privatisation because they are the main users of services. They normally have to pay the rent, arrange for repairs, wait in for gas, electricity and telephone services, deal with children's education, and so on. They also have a wider experience of the health service as it is they who tend to accompany children and relatives when they go for medical treatment.

Shoddy work, delays and cost overruns by private building contractors mean higher rents for council tenants, inconvenience and damage to furniture and fittings as a result of leaking roofs, windows and other defects. Islington Council has used private builders and private architects extensively in its housing programme. A recent study, based on a three-year period up to 1979, showed that shoddy work caused major problems. The council were attempting to sue contractors for over £6 million to recover costs for botched work (a long, slow process). Costs of defects on some estates were enormous—Stock Orchard Crescent £1.47 million, Six Acres Estate £800,000, Marquess Estate £1.25 million. The cost of contracts was £21 million above the original tenders. Half of this was not covered by government housing subsidies. Delays on site cost money as well—the council had to pay the contractor over a longer period and it lost rent and rate income as well as delaying rehousing. In 1977–78 there were average delays of 58 weeks on 32 contracts.

Defects and cost overruns also hit other public services. The Commons Public Accounts Committee reported in July 1982 that more than £30 million worth of 'glaring defects' had been found in 13 new hospitals, all built by contractors.

Less choice. The sale of council housing also has a major effect on tenants and the homeless. Analysis of sales has shown that it is the better-quality houses which are sold. Flats represent less than 2 per cent of sales since 1980. This leads to longer waiting and transfer lists because tenants have a more restricted choice of home and location; higher rents because of discounts on sales, loss of subsidies and high replacement costs; the creation of council ghettos as the flats and unattractive estates are left; and less mobility for tenants. Sales also lead to increased public spending because tax benefits to home owners far outstrip subsidies to council tenants.

Reinforcing the class system. The introduction of education vouchers, described in Chapter 2, is designed to encourage parents to top up their value out of their wages in order to pay for private education. Only the popular schools will survive. Poorer state schools will deteriorate and close to be replaced by new private schools. The children of those who cannot afford to top up their vouchers will be forced to travel further to receive any education at all. Private education reinforces economic and social status and creams off more advantaged children. Fewer working-class people will get into college and university. The student loan scheme will financially cripple those who do get a place.

Parents are already being forced to pay for certain classes, books and equipment. Parents are increasingly decorating and repairing schools on a 'voluntary' basis. A survey of 67 schools by Thurrock Trades Council in 1982 found that one-third of the schools had not been redecorated for over 10 years. There were 27 self-help schemes to repaint and repair schools and maintain footpaths. Seventeen schools relied on private funding for text and library books. Private funding schemes place working-class children at further disadvantage.

Contracting out school cleaning leads to dirtier schools, increased health and safety risks, and less flexibility to organise events after normal hours. Increased cleaning supervision distracts school staff from other duties. A two-year pilot scheme in Lancashire was abandoned in 1973 for these reasons. More recently, a contractor pulled out of a pilot contract in two of Croydon's 154 schools following a stream of complaints from teachers and parents. The education authority had previously lowered cleaning standards in the two schools.

Rigid service. Contractors stick to a literal interpretation of contracts. A recent survey of contractors in NHS ancillary work by the Association of Health Service Treasurers found this often led to demarcation disputes. There were also constant disagreements about standards and level of service. Contractors were reluctant to rectify mistakes or improve standards in case profits suffered. It was often difficult to get rid of an unsatisfactory contractor quickly.

The National Health Service

Market criteria are having a devastating effect on health care and the NHS. Government strategy is to encourage private medicine and a 'partnership' with the NHS while cutting back and reducing NHS services to allow the growth of private health insurance and private hospitals.

Just what this means has been well described by the *Investors' Chronicle* (8 October 1982). 'What's new is the concept of the small commercial hospital. They already exist; they are expected to make money; and they are soon going to be making a lot more.' It went on to describe what makes a hospital commercial:

> Like rears on seats in theatres, it's bodies in beds that count for a private hospital and, preferably bodies which are continually changing.
>
> Commercial hospitals have to be selective about the sort of medical treatment that they offer. Long-stay patients, such as

the elderly, mentally ill and those convalescing do not usually make for good business. What does is the short-stay surgical operation such as hernia repair, varicose vein treatment, removal of tonsils, gall bladder and appendix.

A short stay of an average five days with surgery will ensure that the patient/customer is using the hospital's facilities to the full; accommodation, consultant's fees, anaesthetics, X-rays, blood tests, drugs, etc. Patients who make little demand on surgical services such as those in geriatric wards are simply not cost effective.

So medical services become commodities. Services continue only as long as they are economic.

Private hospitals dealing with routine surgery can be very profitable. The *Financial Times* (12 January 1983) reported that a new hospital in Peterborough is forecasting pre-tax profits of between 25 and 29 per cent in 1983, rising to between 33 and 38 per cent in 1987. Some of the private hospitals in inner London have shown rates of return on capital of up to 30 per cent.

But what does this really mean for the users of the service? We all rely on health care at different times in our lives and at different levels, ranging from check-ups and visits to family doctors to surgery or intensive care following accidents or major illness. It is also a well-documented fact that working-class people of all ages suffer more from illness and accidents than do businesspeople, professionals and managers.

Paying more for less. Hardly a BUPA advertising slogan, but much nearer reality than the usual insurance company sales spiel. A typical private health insurance scheme provides cover, to a certain set limit, for hospital accommodation, doctors' and consultants' fees, drugs, radiotherapy, X-ray and physiotherapy. However, schemes don't generally cover any outpatient care, drugs, dental care, general practice, optical care and other types of treatment. Nor are they liable for the treatment of any disorder which originated before you took out the insurance, unless this was accepted at the time of application. More fundamentally, private insurance fails to provide cover for pregnancy, abortion, vasectomy, accidents, mental handicap, geriatric care, chiropody, osteopathy, psychiatric conditions, or any chronic illness. So you are likely to be faced with substantial additional bills.

You end up paying twice for health care, once through taxation and again through health insurance. The only real benefits are that you can jump the queue for non-urgent operations which can be dealt with quickly and for a set fee. You also gain more privacy, if this is necessary, by obtaining single rooms and other trimmings. It also benefits the rich who can afford to pay the high price of private health care—the cost of a room at the Wellington Hospital in London, owned by the American-based Humana Corporation, is now between £1,200 and £2,030 per week.

Private health insurance has been given the hard sell by many companies, who offer it as part of a wages and conditions package. It is an allowable business expense for tax purposes, but, just as important, firms can ensure that employees get their health treatment at a time most convenient for the company. It also means that workers and management won't have to wait for operations which may cause uncertainty, worry and a reduced commitment to, and output of, work. Health insurance companies offer group schemes to employers which reduce the price from about £350 to about £200 per annum for a young family with two children. There are now 1.8 million subscribers to private health insurance, covering four million people.

There are other costs, too. Health insurance doesn't cover primary care, i.e. visits to general practitioners. While one-third of GPs have private patients, less than 2 per cent have more than 20. The first private family doctor service started in Harrow in late 1982. The initial costs of the service are £65 a year for adults and £52 for children. Home visit fees are £10 for adults and £5 for children. There is also a £10 initial registration fee. Drugs are extra. The combined yearly costs for a family of two adults and two children would on average be at least £625, assuming they were fairly healthy (and that excludes the costs of drugs, dental treatment, eye-tests etc.). Private health care is costly now, and will continue to get more expensive, as insurance premiums are changed annually: BUPA made an operating loss in 1981–82 and had to hike up premiums by 35 per cent in the last half of 1982.

When you're ill, the Tory strategy bites hard. Your earning power is reduced when you're sick, just when you need it most. And if you work for a contractor then paid sickness leave will be less, and for shorter periods. This is the private deal: reduced wages and benefits, larger personal payments to health care, and more voluntary collections to help run and provide hospital facilities. One-third of all personal bankruptcies in the USA are due to failure to pay medical bills.

Profiting from cutting you open. With commercial medicine, it pays to operate. Twice as many operations per head of population take place in the USA as in England and Wales. This is not because people there are less healthy, or that treatment is better or easier to obtain, but because the private health systems means that doctors and surgeons increase their income and profits by carrying out as many operations as possible. It has been estimated that if the eight most common operations were performed in this country as frequently as they were in the USA, the costs would rise from £250 million a year to £630 million a year.

No better treatment but worse to come. There is no evidence that private health care is medically any better; in fact, most doctors argue that the overall quality of the NHS is superior. But the growth of private medicine is likely to lead to a two-tier health care system. It can only grow aided by the systematic attack on the NHS, spending cuts, and hospital and ward closures. Private health is parasitic on the NHS, drawing away its trained staff. Waiting lists will get even longer. This is precisely what is happening already. The Tories don't want to abolish the NHS because the private market simply couldn't take over completely. They do, however, want the NHS to become a second-class, Cinderella service for the chronically sick and ill, children, elderly and working-class people.

Margaret Thatcher claimed that the NHS was 'safe in our hands'—it's about as safe as asking your local butcher to do a heart transplant. This second-class service *will* mean inferior treatment for those unable to afford health insurance and those who are refused treatment by private hospitals. Overcrowded, overworked and often poor-quality public hospitals in the USA are a reminder of the consequences of private medicine. So are the numerous cases of people refused treatment because they don't have health insurance. In one well-publicised case in 1982, a man who'd received serious burns over 95 per cent of his body was refused treatment by 40 American hospitals because he couldn't afford to join his company's £20-a-month scheme. He was eventully flown 600 miles to a hospital in Baltimore, following the intervention of the Governor of Georgia.

Avoid the causes—just blame the individual. Ill-health is caused by many things. Damp, unheated and inadequate housing, unemployment, poverty, pollution, unsafe working conditions— all these are major contributors to illness and injury. They cannot be tackled simply as health problems. The development of a private health care system effectively and conveniently focuses attention away from such matters and deals with health problems in a very narrow commercial relationship between doctor and patient. There needs to be a shift in NHS resources to preventative medicine and primary care, and away from the concentration on high-technology medicine. Private health care will not redress the balance: its profits lie in drugs and operations.

Elderly on the scrap heap. Although the elderly form an increasing proportion of the population, facilities for them are being cut. More elderly people are being forced into private nursing homes, the high fees, conditions and the quality of care and food in which should be a national scandal.

Paying the price for wasted resources. Private health means more paperwork. Insurance schemes are expensive to run because each patient's costs have to be assessed, billed, agreed and paid for every item (pills, drugs, bandages, meals, etc.) and for every service used, including doctors' and consultants' fees. This involves more bureaucracy. The expansion of private medicine means a wasted duplication of resources resulting in more, not less, money being spent in health.

Right-wing advocates of private medicine always point to the 'success' of private health care in the USA. But private medicine covers only 70 per cent of the population and the Federal government has had to introduce Medicare and Medicaid schemes for the elderly and the poor who can't afford health insurance. Medicare alone cost the government £30,000 million in 1982, and it is expected to double in the next five years. Hospital bills vary by thousands of dollars for the same operation. Now some states are trying to standardise costs. New York wants to put surcharges on Blue Cross (the main insurance scheme), Medicare, and Medicaid in order to create a fund to rescue public hospitals from bankruptcy. These hospitals take care of one million New Yorkers who can't afford insurance, but who are not poor enough to qualify for Medicaid. Most health care research is funded by the Federal government.

The American dream: contracting nightmare

The effects of privatisation can already be clearly seen in developments in the United States. The 1983 US budget includes £85 billion for consultants and contracting out of Federal work, and the Reagan administration has consistently attempted to make it easier to contract out government work. The USA has about 2.9 million Federal employees. But a further four million are employed in a 'phantom government', comprising consultants and contractors on Federal contracts. State governments also employ consultants and contractors. In 1980, Ohio spent £30 million in this way. The Wisconsin Legislature Fiscal Bureau identified 1,056 contracts current in 1981. They were valued at £165 million.

Contracting out of local government services has increased in recent years following a whole series of tax cut campaigns in several states and cities. Architectural and engineering services, refuse collection, highway construction, building repair, ambulance and legal services are services most often contracted out. However, there are hundreds of very small townships and school districts even within the large metropolitan areas in the USA. Surveys have shown that contracting out is twice as high in towns with under 10,000 population compared to larger cities.

'It is getting to be one of the rituals of spring—baseball, cherry blossoms, and General Accounting Office reports on consulting waste, ' said Representative Geraldine Ferraro, opening hearings on the Consulting Reform and Disclosure Act, House of Representatives, on 6 May 1982.

Three recent studies by the GAO revealed massive abuses by consultants and contractors. Sixty-eight per cent of 444 Environmental Protection Agency contracts were modified to increase costs and extend time limits. The original cost soared by 150 per cent to £205 million. An investigation of 256 Department of Defense contracts discovered that many were taking over departmental functions which were 'weakening its [the department's] ability to perform in-house work essential to fulfilment of its defense mission'. In 1980, all but one of 111 contracts in six Federal agencies uncovered problems of waste.

Many contracts were awarded to ex-government officials who went to work for the consultants they were responsible for monitoring. A *Washington Post* investigation in June 1980 found that nearly 70 per cent of 16,101 research and consulting contracts were awarded without competition.

All these investigations exposed widespread conflicts of interest. For example, the government has awarded multi-million dollar contracts to major oil and chemical companies and their research

divisions, such as Exxon, Monsanto and Dow, to provide and
evaluate data used in regulating their own products. Many other
contracts were never completed. The end product of others were
classified as useless. The *Washington Post* interviewed 600 government officials and contractors. It discovered widespread corruption: entertainment, sex and favours were used to get or to
retain contracts.

Government departments often didn't have enough staff to
monitor contracts effectively. There are also longer-term problems
because

> firms often develop expertise and an 'institutional' memory
> for a government agency, making themselves indispensable.
> The result is that agencies grow to depend on consulting firms
> regardless of their cost and find it difficult to break away
> (*Midwest Monitor*, Midwest Center for Public Sector Labor
> Relations, September 1980).

In 1979 lawyers from the Federal government's Justice Department began what appeared to be a routine investigation into the
bidding activities of road contractors in Tennessee and Virginia.
By 1982 it had grown into the largest anti-trust case in American
history. 'Operation Roadrunner' has grand juries sitting in 17
states examining corrupt practices and hundreds of millions of
dollars in illegal profits. So far, 156 corporations and 186 individuals have been charged on tender rigging, mail fraud and
perjury—the vast majority have pleaded guilty. More than £20
million has been paid in fines.

British readers may be reminded of the corruption trials and
imprisonment of architect John Poulson and councillor Dan Smith
in the 1970s, which resulted from swindles in contracting out public
work.

6.

Public Services—In Whose Interest?

There has been too little debate about the problems of working in and using public services. We need a much wider understanding in the labour movement about the contradictions within the welfare state—its good and bad points—and the underlying causes. It is only on this basis that we can understand why the Tories have been able to get away with their savage attacks on jobs and services in the public sector.

The threat of privatisation and spending cuts forces us to defend our jobs and services. But defensive action has to be honest: it has to admit that there are deficiencies in the quality and level of provision and to make these central to a positive strategy for improved and expanded services.

The trade union movement has rarely argued for the merits of public service, nor has it developed a comprehensive policy on what kind of services we need and want. All too often, there are demands for further nationalisation of industries and services or for increased spending on housing and health. These are important demands but, in isolation, they are very inadequate.

This chapter starts with a brief history of some of the main services, outlining their origins in the private or public sector, and the reasons for the takeover by the state. It also examines the role of the public sector in the economy. This is followed by an analysis of the positive and negative aspects of public services run by a capitalist state. The final section identifies the main advantages of public services over the private sector.

Origins of the public sector

Many services started life in the private sector. Yet we have come to expect to use the NHS, gas, water, electricity, schools and colleges when we need them. With the government now hell bent on privatisation, it is important to remind ourselves why and how our services became public.

Council housing

The first national subsidised housebuilding programme was undertaken in 1919. It promised to provide 500,000 'Homes fit for Heroes' within three years. During the nineteenth century, housing had been mainly in the hands of private landlords. There was a constant housing shortage, and the houses which were built were of a desperately low standard. The Victorian do-gooders who were prepared to accept lower profits had faded from the scene, and public health legislation failed miserably to cope with the problem.

Before the first world war, only a few councils were building homes for working people. The first rent control, the Rent Restriction Act, was introduced in 1915 as a consequence of the famous Clydeside rent strike which involved tenants and workers in the Glasgow munitions factories. The post-war period saw widespread unrest and militancy, and growing threats of working-class action over bad housing conditions and high rents. Returning servicemen began to squat empty properties. Government inquiries began to recommend state intervention in housing.

Another factor was the growth of other forms of investment which didn't carry similar responsibilities to housing management. Industrial investment had become more profitable after tax changes in 1878 and, particularly after 1904, there was a massive shift of money out of the country as Britain expanded its foreign investments. Investment in housing declined and housebuilding fell from 150,000 in 1903 to 45,000 in 1914. This in turn increased the pressure from the building industry for large contracts and a steady flow of work.

Since 1919 council housing has had a history of spending cuts and changes in the amount and system of subsidies. Some governments have built for general housing needs, others have simply replaced houses lost through slum clearance. Annual completions reached a peak of nearly 270,000 in the mid-1950s. Rent increases have sparked many important rent strikes over the years.

Direct Labour Organisations (DLOs)

First set up in 1892, these local authority building departments have come under attack whenever the private sector in construction has suffered a fall in demand. The first DLO was set up by the

London County Council in response to corruption scandals and complaints about shoddy work. Building workers were also well organised at the time and fighting for better wages and conditions. Unemployment was high and DLOs were seen as a way of creating useful jobs. Other local authorities followed. Seventy new DLOs were established in the first year of the 1919 national council housebuilding programme. When housebuilding slumped, in 1927, the National Federation of Building Trades Employers (NFBTE) was quick to attack 'the menace of direct labour', attempting to show that DLOs were expensive and inefficient.

The number of DLOs doubled after the second world war. However, another recession in the building industry in the late 1950s brought more attacks, and the Ministry of Housing stipulated that DLOs would, in future, have to compete with private builders for every third contract. In 1967, the DLO workforce reached an all-time high of 200,000, of whom about one-fifth were employed on new construction work. During the property boom of the early 1970s, many local authorities found difficulty in getting private builders to tender for council housebuilding: office and shopping centre developments were more profitable. But the boom ended and cuts in public spending on new housing, schools and hospitals followed. The NFBTE and other building employers' organisations again campaigned against Direct Labour Organisations, attempting both to gain more work and to scuttle Labour's plans for increased public ownership of the building industry. After its election in 1979, the Tory government responded with new stringent controls on DLOs.

Electricity and gas

Both local government and private companies provided electricity and gas, until their nationalisation in 1948 and 1949 respectively.

The London and Westminster Gas Light and Coke Company set up the first gas works in 1812. By 1830 there were 200 gas undertakings, often competing with each other: eight companies, each with a main down either side of the street, were competing for business in the Strand in London. Manchester Corporation was the first council to run a gas undertaking, and others soon followed either by buying private companies or by setting up new undertakings. By the early 1880s, one-third of the 500 statutory undertakings were municipally owned, a ratio which was maintained until nationalisation.

Expansion in gas continued up to 1939, but at a decreased rate because of the competition from electricity. The government-appointed Heyworth Committee recommended public ownership.

> Few people would disagree that in the mid-1940s the UK gas industry with its multiplicity of undertakings—334 of which had a capital of less than £20,000—its varying standards of gas quality and service, etc., would benefit from some measure of rationalisation and the establishment of larger more efficient entities. (Malcolm Peebles, *Evolution of the Gas Industry*, Macmillan, 1980)

The gas companies didn't even campaign against public ownership because they were well compensated. From 1949 to 1960 a modernisation programme included laying 21,200 miles of new mains; 622 old and inefficient gasworks were closed.

Electric arc lamps were first used for lighting public places from the early 1860s. The Stock Market boom of 1882, combined with often exaggerated and fraudulent claims about the future of electric light, saw shares soar in electricity companies. The same year introduced the Electricity Lighting Act which prevented a private monopoly being established, imposed maximum prices and allowed local authorities to purchase electricity companies after 21 years, later extended to 42.

A few towns (e.g. Sheffield and Brighton) had electric street lighting, but most early developments were confined to the wealthy parts of London. Gas was much cheaper. Bradford was the first local authority to set up a municipal electricity undertaking, in 1889. Although others followed, private companies remained dominant and pressure groups like the Industrial Freedom League and the Liberty and Property Defence League agitated against municipal enterprise. By 1903, municipal undertakings accounted for two-thirds of all connections to the public supply mains.

A survey of 300 electricity supply undertakings in 1910–12 showed that municipalities sold more electricity and sold it more cheaply (47 per cent less) than private companies; they also had lower capital and working costs. The need for economies of scale, improved load factors and a national transmission network to cover breakdowns led Baldwin's Conservative government to establish the Central Electricity Board in 1926. Its role was also to impose a uniform supply voltage as manufacturers had to make a variety of domestic appliances. Full public ownership followed in 1948; over £542 million was paid in compensation, mainly to the companies.

Railways

By 1920 there were still over 120 companies operating railways. Aggressive expansion in the nineteenth century had led to many problems. Expansion was often at the expense of consolidating and improving the existing network. Technical progress was inhibited by the power complex of railway leaders and the private wagon owners, as Derek Aldcroft and Harry Richardson show in their study, *The British Economy, 1870–1939*:

> No other country allowed the riot of individuality to occur with regard to the different types of axle boxes, tyres, springs and handbrakes. British railways had no less than 200 types of axle boxes and over 40 variations of the ordinary wagon handbrake.

Following government control during the first world war, nationalisation was rejected. However, the Railways Act 1921 did amalgamate all the companies into four large groups: the London and North Eastern; Southern; Great Western; and London, Midland and Scottish. This was completed within two years, but lack of investment, economic recessions in the 1920s and 1930s, and increasing competition from the motor car and road haulage meant that rail traffic did not reach its 1913 level until after the second world war.

Health

Being poor and ill in the early nineteenth century meant a visit to the workhouse infirmary. The wealthier were cared for in the pay beds of voluntary or teaching hospitals. A series of investigations exposed the stark reality of workhouse conditions and led to some reforms, including the establishment of small outpatient clinics in larger voluntary hospitals. General practitioners operated on traditional business principles, setting fees on the basis of market forces. In the northern coalfields a 'club' system developed whereby a levy on wages paid for hiring doctors and, in some cases, building cottage hospitals.

The first national insurance scheme was started by the government in 1911. Administered by the insurance companies, it provided free consultation and free medicine from GPs—but only for wage earners. Local authorities also set up more welfare services, including school meals and medicals. Nevertheless, up until one year before their takeover by local authorities, in 1929, there were still over half a million people in Poor Law hospitals (which had increasingly replaced workhouse infirmaries). Over 35,000 were still in workhouses. At a time of rife poverty and unemployment, debt collectors were employed to extract doctors' fees. Medical and surgical advances took a long time to benefit working-class patients.

The NHS was set up in 1948. It was to be financed by general taxation and free at the time of use. Voluntary hospitals came under public ownership. But there were still fundamental flaws. Top doctors were bought off by special payments and privileges, and consultants were allowed to continue private practice within the NHS.

This brief history shows that it wasn't simply the failure of the private market to supply and run services at reasonable cost to working-class people which led to public services. Working-class struggle played an important role. So did the demands of capital for national markets and a co-ordinated transport network. The state increasingly took over responsibility to provide industry with an adequately housed, educated and healthy workforce.

Public spending since the war

There has been a rapid growth in public services and public spending over the last 35 years, both in Britain and in other countries. Contrary to right-wing propaganda, this did not come about as a result of prodigal councils, waste, or collectivist attitudes. Rather, its cause lies in several fundamental changes in British society.

First, the demographic changes. The population has increased by six million since 1945. There have also been radical changes in the age-structure of the population. The high post-war birth rate created a need for more schools, colleges and universities. At the other end of the scale, between 1951 and 1980, the number of people over the age of 65 rose by more than 50 per cent. This has meant extra health and social service staff and facilities, and more sheltered accommodation.

Second, the capitalist economy has itself caused a growth in social needs. With unemployment five times greater now than it was 10 years ago, 4.5 million people are dependent on unemployment and social security benefits. The other social costs of mass redundancies and closures must also be met. Redevelopment and property schemes spell displacement to more and more tenants.

Supplying the needs of people costs money; improving the quality and/or range of services available to them costs more because caring cannot be done by machines. ﹒

The third major change had been in the role of the state. Its spending has increased in line with its growing responsibility for the care of the population. It now also provides grants to industry, industrial sites and factories, and increasing grants and subsidies to home owners. The state is still compensating for the failures of the private sector: it inherited: investment-starved industries, a neglected railway system, and old school and hospital buildings. Today, investment in new buildings remains far short of requirements.

Many of these recent changes would not have occurred without constant labour movement demands for new and better services. Lower teacher–pupil or doctor–patient ratios, more nurseries and so on cannot be achieved on the cheap. Yet, both Labour and Tory governments have imposed massive cuts from the mid-seventies onwards.

In whose interests?

It is no coincidence that this has happened in a recession. Now capital needs to regain control over the profitable parts of services and a greater share of the work supplying public services in order to maintain profitability. The capitalist system seeks to legitimate itself when it is most under question. By launching a privatisation campaign on the premise that the private sector is better than the public sector, the state helps to retain confidence in the capitalist economy.

There are other longer-term economic concerns. The government's think tank report on the future of the welfare state expressed concern about demographic changes and their effects on public services at a time of no or slow economic growth. The 1981 Census showed that nearly 1 million more people became pensioners between 1971 and 1981. There was a 10 per cent drop in the number of people under 16 years of age. This trend is expected to continue and has major implications for pensions, health and social service spending. Public spending's share of GDP is estimated to rise from the present 45 per cent to 60 per cent by 1990 (although Sweden and Holland are already above this level). Faced with increasing costs, governments in various European countries have been cutting back public spending, transferring responsibility and costs to individuals.

Privatisation is also symptomatic of capital's changing requirements. Healthy and well-educated workers were essential to the reconstruction of the post-war economy. Now, with capitalism in its technological phase, it can dispense with a large proportion of the workforce. The welfare state has served its purpose.

Getting rid of a universal system of welfare has advantages to capital. It reduces costs and taxes, and opens up markets for firms to profiteer in private education and health. At the same time, privatised services will still supply sufficient educated and healthy workers for what jobs there are. For those not able to buy their way into jobs—tough! It's clear from this scenario what the position would be for most working-class people.

This involves remoulding services and reshaping relations between the state, unions and users. This includes dividing working-class groups and interests which have developed as a result of the welfare state. Privatisation generates conflicting interests between council tenants and those who have bought their homes. Some trade unionists have private health insurance, others do not. Some employees buy shares in the company, others refuse to. With workers and users having virtually no control over services, contradictory forces operating continuously, and a Labour Party committed to a mixed economy and 'socialist' welfare state, it is not surprising that the Tories have been able to get away with such an extensive privatisation strategy.

However, while it is one thing to support public services in *principle*, our experience in *practice*, both as workers and users, often leads to a major questioning of these political ideals. Labour history portrays nationalisation and more public services as unambiguous gains by the labour movement. It is not so simple.

Contradictory heritage

The way services are now organised and run makes it often seem as if they are working against us, not for us. There are five main contradictions about public services and the welfare state.

First, while the state provides services which people need, and which they help to pay for through taxes and rates, we are made to feel guilty and branded as scroungers living off the state when we use these services. We usually have to undergo a rigorous examination before we get them.

Council housing, for example, wasn't originally intended for working-class people alone. Its function was to provide good quality houses at reasonable rents for all. Over the years, however, it has been stigmatised as catering only for the poor or for the loonies who don't want to become property owners. A lot of council housing is well built and designed, often to a higher standard than private housing. True, there are also a lot of drab, defective, concrete estates suffering from neglect and disrepair. However, this 'decline' does not signify anything inherently wrong with council housing. The problems come because, ever since its inception, it has operated within the context of the private market.

Private financiers, private landowners, private architects and private builders have consistently exploited council housing. Although the pooling and sharing of all the costs remains socialist in principle, most other aspects of management are not.

Some council tenants now face the ultimate rip-off. Government-enforced rent increases have created a surplus in some councils' Housing Revenue Accounts. Cambridgeshire and Havering have transferred this surplus—£3 million in two years in Havering's case—to the general rates fund to hold down rate increases for industry and owner occupiers.

Because housing is provided by the council the local state gets most of the blame for any problems. It masks the real role of the private sector landowners, financiers, architects and builders. Increasingly welfare provision is designed to pressure tenants to become homeowners, to act as a form of deterrent to keep people 'working' the capitalist system, and to provide a last resort for those who fail.

Similarly, while unemployment and social security payments represent a 'gain' for working-class people, the state and its friends ensure that take-up is allied to maximum oppression. Many benefits have low take-up rates. Those who do claim benefit are made to feel 'ashamed' to do so. The state also regulates the level of benefits based on the needs of capital for labour. Yet the state doles out millions of pounds to business and industry in the form of grants, subsidies and other handouts. Rent-free businesses in development areas are one thing, rent-free tenants are another.

Second, services are organised and run in a way that denies class identity and any collective response. In fact, the state will often go to great lengths to prevent users organising. When tenants and claimants organise, the state often responds in one of two ways. It may deny the right to organise collectively and refuse to 'recognise' the organisation. Or maybe the authority will try to incorporate the organisation into the state through sharing responsibility. While the state funds community workers, ostensibly to help organise tenants' organisations and other collective action, their training and education makes it likely that they will adopt an establishment point of view: many community workers will help to control and dampen militancy. Various bodies, such as Community Health Councils, have been set up to channel users' complaints; they have little real power. This is not to tar everybody with the same brush. Some state-funded organisations have backed militant action. So have many state workers as part of their trade union and labour movement activities.

Third, workers in the public services are divided and separated from the users whom they are, in theory, providing the service for.

Despite the fact that these workers are also *users* of services the state has ensured that they identify with the services almost entirely in terms of employment. There are a number of reasons for this. Services are provided *for* people and not *with* them. Some services, such as gas, water and electricity, have very little direct contact with the public. The labour movement has failed to mount an effective fight for control of services and the ideology of trade unionism has, in a sense, assisted the state in maintaining divisions. There are, of course, some real conflicts of interest between workers and users. Industrial action often means a reduced or withdrawn service. However, the state, the media and the right exploit these divisions: they did this very visibly when the health workers were on strike in 1982, and during the water workers' dispute of 1983. The Tories identify and exaggerate many of the problems of public services in order to encourage dissatisfaction and therefore greater use of private services. This makes alliances between workers and users more difficult to organise. Privatisation is putting public service jobs and the quality of services at stake, yet the Tories' propaganda tries to hide the fact that public service workers are also taxpayers, ratepayers and often rentpayers as well.

Fourth, the state provides services which are needed by working-class people but in a form often designed to meet the needs of capital and to reinforce belief in the existing economic system.

For example, transport systems are based overwhelmingly on the need to get people to and from work. Hence the low priority given to certain routes and to off-peak services when those with responsibility for shopping or looking after children are more likely to need them.

Fifth, while the expansion of public services has resulted, until recently, in more jobs and improved working conditions, many workers in the services receive low pay and little recognition.

Public services are run along capitalist forms of control and organisation. The employer–employee relationship is really no different from its counterpart in the private sector. Better conditions and benefits had to be fought for, they were not handed down through the benevolence of the state. Basic wages often have to be supplemented with income from shift work and overtime. Many workers now have little responsibility or job satisfaction. Less care and lower standards are the inevitable results.

The case for public services

Whilst there are many contradictions and problems for both workers and users of public services in a capitalist economy, it is important not to let these problems overwhelm us. We should not be blind to the very real advantages of public services, even in their present form.

* Public services are aimed at meeting social needs, not the demands of the marketplace and private profits.

* Public services are provided to meet the needs of everybody. Private firms provide only for those who can afford it.

* Public services can distribute resources between areas more fairly. Heavily used sections of services can offset higher unit costs of lower levels of usage in other areas. The market mechanism cannot allocate resources more fairly. It is based on a system for which those with resources get more—the wealthier get wealthier. Firms go where they judge there is a market. Poorer and rural areas suffer as a consequence.

* Public services make people's needs matters of public concern. Privatisation individualises needs, and absolves us from our collective responsibility to identify them and to monitor the adequacy of provision.

* Public services are accountable directly to the public through council committees and elections, although the system is still in-

adequate. However, the potential exists for public service workers and users to gain more control over running services, by democratising management and working through joint committees with councillors to decide policies. Private firms are accountable only to their shareholders; a few directors decide their policy. In multinational companies decisions are often not even made in Britain.

* Public service accounts are usually open to inspection. You can get a lot of detailed information about local government expenditure. The private sector only has to satisfy company law. It's virtually impossible to get similar information about companies.

* Public services are often able to achieve a high standard of service. They can be more responsive and flexible to changing circumstances. Profits determine the quality of work for private firms—they are much more likely to cut corners, do patch up repairs and use inferior materials.

* Public services can often achieve higher standards of employment than private firms. The public sector usually gives greater stability of employment; stronger trade union organisation; better pay, pensions, holidays and sickness benefits; and better working conditions, including health and safety.

* Public services provide extensive teaching and training in health, education, construction and other services which benefit workers and users. The expansion of private health and education has only been possible by firms poaching trained staff from the NHS and education authorities. Contractors provide little or no training.

* Public services can be more effective and give better value for money than the private sector. Public bodies give continuity of service, whereas private firms often abandon contracts through financial problems or bankruptcy or simply leave at the end of the contract period.

* Public services are usually cheaper for the same range and quality of services and the same pay, benefits and working conditions. Private firms can usually only undercut the cost of public services by employing fewer workers, with lower pay, inferior benefits and longer hours; or by increasing charges for users; or by using public facilities such as depots and repair services at subsidised rates.

* Payment for public services through taxes and rates is fairer and cheaper than paying directly from your pocket every time you

use them. No one likes paying higher taxes and rates, but the alternative is the introduction of higher and new charges for services, and various new insurance schemes to cover ill-health and other eventualities.

* Public services can be less wasteful than the private market. There is waste in the public services—but less than in the private sector (see Chapter 3).

7.

A Political Strategy for Public Services

Privatisation is a *political* attack. It is a means of plundering public sector assets and redistributing wealth to the wealthy and to industry and commerce. But it is more than an attack on public spending and workers' conditions; it is also an attack on trade unionism.

The public services are increasingly becoming the key arena of class struggle. Tory strategy now focuses on massive public sector job losses. The privatisation of health, housing, education and social services will lead to a big cut in living standards for workers, pensioners and the unemployed. Yet the public sector can play a crucial part in creating socially useful jobs. Because of decline and massive job loss in manufacturing industry, it is also where the main political and economic strength of the trade union movement lies. A weakened trade union movement will have knock-on effects, reducing the relative strength of trades councils, making it more difficult to build an effective women's movement in the unions and restraining the relationship with the Labour Party.

How can the labour movement reverse privatisation and improve and expand public services? What strategies are needed to fight the ideological battle, the multinational contractors and right-wing pressure groups? And how can this challenge be mounted when the trade union movement is weakened by Tory anti-union legislation, propaganda, and falling membership?

This chapter analyses and draws out the lessons from recent campaigns agains privatisation and the strategy adopted by the unions nationally, the Trades Union Congress (TUC) and the Labour party. It outlines a general strategy to fight privatisation. This strategy has to focus on workers' and users' control of services, and the need to restructure the old welfare state on working-class terms. It discusses the limits of trade unionism and the changes necessary to fight privatisation, including the forging of much stronger international links. Finally, drawing on the lessons learnt from campaigns against cuts in public spending since 1975, it spells out organising and action strategies. This is followed in Chapter 8 with a seven-point plan detailing specific organising and action tactics for activists in areas directly affected.

All-out negotiating

Present action against privatisation can be divided into three broad categories: negotiating, tendering and industrial action.

First, many workers and trade union officials have tried to negotiate a way out by offering cuts in direct labour. Authorities have often proposed cuts based on contractors' crude estimates or some other pie-in-the-sky figure. Armed with detailed costings of the direct labour service, shop stewards and union officials have suggested savings which frequently include cuts in jobs, vehicles and so on. This has often succeeded in retaining the work in the public sector. There have, on the other hand, been instances of unions preparing alternative money-saving schemes to extend or alter services which do not jeopardise the workforce in this way.

The hard reality of the present economic and political climate is that some reorganisation of services and changes in certain procedures and practices cannot always be avoided. But reasonable settlements cannot be achieved by relying solely on negotiations.

Some authorities are committed to privatisation irrespective of the consequences. Others are less dogmatic. There are often conflicting interests and views within authorities. However, it would be wrong to get optimistic on the strength of differences between 'wet' and Thatcherite Tories.

Second, some workers have submitted tenders where the authority has been committed to privatisation in principle. Refuse workers in Birmingham submitted a tender alongside Pritchard's and other contractors. They won the contract but lost 263 jobs. Those who kept their jobs had a 40 per cent workload increase. There had been differences between the unions on strategy. NALGO blacked work on the preparation of contract documents, but the manual workers, supported by the TGWU and GMBATU, decided to submit a tender. Similar tactics are being used to try to retain school cleaning work in Birmingham.

Third, there have been various forms of industrial action. In

Wandsworth, there was a six-week strike by NUPE and GMBATU refuse workers, supported by selective action by NAL-GO workers, a local publicity campaign and some solidarity action from neighbouring boroughs. This failed to prevent contractors taking over. Meanwhile, in Bury, an 18-month campaign, orga-nised by a joint union committee, has stopped, at least for the present, the privatisation of refuse, street cleaning and vehicle maintenance.

There have also been one-day stoppages by British Telecom workers. Eight unions opposing the sale of gas showrooms were supported by British Gas Corporation, consumer groups, and gas appliance manufacturers worried about a drop in demand and increased imports. Their fight is often cited as a successful cam-paign. However, it only postponed the possible sale because the Oil and Gas (Enterprise) Act 1982 gave the government power to enforce it.

Limits of co-operatives and workers' buy-outs

A few workers in the public services have suggested setting up a workers' co-operative as a response to the threat of privatisation and it is worth looking at this kind of proposal in some detail. It would involve workers in a particular service or department setting up an organisation which they would own and control to compete for the contract from the council. But this response is unsatisfac-tory. In order to compete with contractors, workers would have to take responsibility for cutting their own wages, benefits and condi-tions. Setting up a co-operative doesn't alter this basic feature of privatisation. Because of this the local authority still achieves its aims. It would only be concerned about getting the job done for a certain price and it would have got rid of its responsibility for conditions of employment. In this situation it is largely a defensive tactic. Setting up a co-operative does nothing to help the public sector tackle many of the existing problems. For example, it does nothing to make public services more democratic because provi-sion is taken right out of the public sector.

Setting up a co-operative to bid alongside contractors is a diver-sion from the struggle to retain the work within the public sector. Any worker involved would be under great pressure to refrain from action during a campaign against privatisation.

Co-operatives would have to compete against multinational

companies, which have the resources to invest and reinvest in new equipment and obtain economies of scale by buying materials in vast quantities.

Co-operatives do not challenge the way the private market operates nor the power of the big companies and financial institutions. They represent a different way of organising workers and, at least in theory, give a greater sense of job satisfaction and control. In reality, workers would have to cut down on the same items as the companies they would be competing against. They are likely to achieve less real workers' control than the workers within public service.

There are examples of housing co-operative alternatives outside of the public sector. These have diverted both attention and money away from dealing with the real problems of council housing. A repeat of this pattern in other public services would have major implications for both workers and users.

Workers in sections of nationalised industries have suggested a worker buy-out. The National Freight Corporation example was noted in Chapter 2. Many of the objections to co-operatives also apply to worker buy-outs. Without the support of financial institutions, a worker buy-out would not be able to raise sufficient capital for investment in new plant and equipment. With such support, financial institutions will want to safeguard their money by demanding a role in decision-making through share ownership. Furthermore, workers would face a conflict of interest being both employees and shareholders (see Chapter 3). Their savings would also be at risk.

Clearly, co-operatives and buy-outs face major problems because they operate in a capitalist economy. They are not really an alternative to privatisation because, practically and ideologically, they fit into the Tories' plans to dismantle large chunks of the public sector.

These arguments apply particularly strongly where workers are prepared to take on extra responsibilities and consent to the use of volunteers—for medical ancillary services, for example. In effect these feed straight into the kind of privatisation pushed by the Tories under their motion of 'community care'.

The trade union response

The TUC Public Services Committee is supposed to be running a campaign against privatisation. Early in 1982 it produced a rather drab leaflet outlining some of the disadvantages of contracting out. The minutes of the 12 October 1982 Committee meeting reveal the sense of urgency and importance attached to this campaign.

> The Committee discussion centred on the appropriate tactics for the campaign against privatisation. Reference was made to the conclusion of both the Nationalised Industries Committee and the Economic Committee that priority should be given to campaigning against specific acts of privatisation rather than to a generalised campaign against the concept of privatisation.
>
> After further discussion it was agreed that a circular should be sent to unions requesting information on privatisation so that a draft statement could be prepared for the next meeting of the committee.

At national level, union action has rarely gone beyond leaflets and information in union journals. However, NUPE national office and the London Division produced education packs on privatisation for a series of educational workshops for shop stewards. The 1982 NUPE Conference passed resolutions supporting the Wandsworth struggle and instructed the Executive Council to co-ordinate and initiate action at all levels against privatisation. There were similar anti-privatisation resolutions at other union Conferences. The union conference boycott of Blackpool, where the council was planning to contract out refuse services, indicated further possibilities for action. But action has failed to live up to many shop stewards' expectations.

NALGO launched a £1 million publicity campaign in spring 1983 to 'defend the public services'. While it is laudable that NALGO should have allocated so much money to its campaign, it is a tragic mistake to limit it to 'defence' and a public relations exercise involving carnivals, competitions and adverts.

Some trade unions (for example, TGWU, UCATT and GMBATU) have members in both the private and public sectors. NUPE, POEU and NALGO have members only in the public sector, although NALGO is considering extending membership to the private sector. Others may follow.

Union responses to privatisation have varied. The POEU is opposed to Project Mercury but ASTMS has given it tacit support. Within British Telcom, there have been differences between the POEU and UCW on strategies to fight privatisation. Because

Project Mercury is to lay its cables alongside British Rail's tracks the NUR sees the potential for additional members to offset those lost by redundancies on the railways. Clearly, the scene is set for more conflict on strategies on how to fight privatisation and on unionising privatised sections. The danger is that this is seen primarily as a numbers game because the decrease in union membership during the recession has put unions under increasing financial pressure.

Labouring

The Labour Party's Alternative Economic Strategy commits it to some form of renationalisation and expansion of public services. Labour's 1982 programme states:

> We will thus return all industrial assets sold off by the Tories into public ownership at the earliest opportunity; We will restore the public monopoly in the field of post and telecommunications and return 'Project Mercury' to British Telecom; and restore the rights of the British Gas Corporation and British National Oil Corporation.

It also calls for an extension of the public sector to include profitable firms in key sectors of industry, together with substantial changes to public corporations, such as improved industrial democracy and agreed development plans.

Assets will be taken back into public ownership without full compensation—shareholders will receive precisely what they paid for the shares at the time of denationalisation. (The Labour Party Conference 1981 had called for renationalisation *without compensation*.)

The programme also calls for the separation of private health from the NHS by removing all pay beds, and for the takeover of parts of the private health sector which can be used to meet local health needs. These and other points in the programme make for encouraging but deceptive reading. First, they are Labour Party policy but do not necessarily commit a Labour government to implement them. Second, the past experience of Labour governments and the scale of privatisation question just how far renationalisation and the takeover of private health and education will be implemented. Third, despite good intentions about reorganising services it is likely that these objectives will get lost in the struggle to return them to the public sector at all.

All the variations of the AES and the TUC's alternative strategy call for increased public spending. Increased public spending is seen more in terms of what it can do for the economy (by boosting employment) and British industry than for its benefits to public services. Clearly, spending more in the same old way will achieve little beyond some job creation. The proposed focus on capital spending will mean more contracts for industry. And what qualitative differences will result from further nationalisation and the renationalisation of assets already sold off? Simply expanding public services as they presently stand is not socialism. It is subject to all the contradictions examined in Chapter 6—contradictions which have done so much to discredit the very concept of public provision of services.

Learning the hard way

There are a number of important lessons from recent struggles against privatisation. First, since it is a political attack it must be met by a political response from the labour movement. Struggles to date have shown that traditional trade union economism will not stop privatisation. The shedding of jobs compensated by higher productivity and bonuses is, at best, a temporary holding operation. Employers will invariably return for more, and privatisation will rear its ugly head again. Trying to outbid the contractors means getting locked into a job-loss–wage-cutting downward spiral. This 'efficiency' plays right into the Tories' hands. It can also delude those workers who retain their jobs that a few extra pounds a week will protect them from the impact of privatisation, which extends far beyond their workplace.

Second, industrial action alone is inadequate. Escalating strike action will not necessarily increase the possibility of winning a campaign. Because privatisation is a political attack, it is essential to organise, build support and take direct action with the users of services. Occupation and demonstrations can be as important to a campaign as the withdrawal of labour.

Third, there is an urgent need for co-ordinated national action to oppose privatisation in principle and to support local or specific campaigns. The absence of a nationwide counter-response to the Tories' ideological onslaught has been widely felt. It would also help to overcome isolation and tackle multinational companies.

Fourth, strategies must recognise the problems in the public services—there is a lot wrong with many services and there always will be as long as they operate in a capitalist economy. We have to develop a better understanding of the contradictions and to politicise them.

These lessons must be combined with those learnt from the cuts campaigns since 1975. Campaigns drew together public service unions, tenants and community groups, Trades Councils and women's organisations. Action included several hospital and nursery occupations and work-ins, marches and demonstrations. They emphasised the importance of links between workers and users, the advantages of organising political action in combination with traditional trade union tactics, and the need for democratic control of campaigns. New organisational strategies drew in many more women than would otherwise have been involved and this led to several lively campaigns.

Cuts campaigns also showed that defensive demands alone are insufficient. They are usually limited to restoring things which were already inadequate. In addition, many people will not take part in action to defend services, although they support them in principle, because they regularly experience alienation, excessive red tape and long delays. They don't experience public services as *their* services. A defensive response, inadequate between 1975 and '80, is even more inadequate now under the Tories' political and ideological attack. In addition, the demands and tactics used by the trade union movement in the 1960s when public services were expanding are now inadequate in a period of mass unemployment and privatisation. The well-tried tactics to fight for economic issues in a period of capitalist expansion are found wanting when capital is clawing back wages, lowering benefits, worsening conditions and shedding jobs.

Developing visions and alternatives about what public services should be like must also play a crucial role. Cuts campaigns exposed the lack of such debate and discussion on any significant scale in the labour movement.

Cuts campaigns and the 1982 NHS dispute also showed that national campaigns lose impetus when they are regionalised.

A more fundamental question is whether the struggle will be constrained by the limits of trade unionism. Can public sector workers develop consciousness which extends beyond trade union consciousness—one which includes workers' interests and the range and quality of services for themselves and other users? This does not deny the centrality of jobs, wages and conditions for trade unionists. But a stronger *political* consciousness is needed which encompasses workplace, service and outside issues. Only by moving beyond a strictly trade union consciousness can we develop joint action and alliances with the users of services. Faced with the multinationals' financial resources, diversity of products and services, structure, centralised control and political power, the trade union movement must build greater unity and co-operation between public sector unions. More analysis of multinationals' activities is also essential. Stronger links are needed with public sector unions in Europe, the USA and other countries, to draw on lessons learnt there from campaigns against privatisation and successes in regaining work for the public sector.

Fighting for control

Despite gaining more jobs, better working conditions and more public services over the last 35 years the labour movement has not gained any real *control* over the running and quality of, or investment in, public services. Workers' ideas of how to improve and expand services have, all too often, lain dormant because there were no means to develop and implement them on their terms, or they were too easily exploited by and credited to management— the 'good ideas' boxes. Users' ideas were often met with hostility from workers because there was no common basis to hammer out problems and conflicting interests.

There are few proposals for industrial democracy in the public services. The recent TUC/Labour Party Liaison Committee *Report on Planning and Industrial Democracy* said virtually nothing about democracy, control and planning in the public sector. It referred back to a three-page 1977 report. Relying solely on accountability to MPs and councillors has clearly been shown to be inadequate. Ideally, a system of industrial democracy would include workers' and users' involvement in planning and running services, collectively redefining social and economic needs. This must go hand in hand with the struggle for democratic control of trades unions.

Full control on our terms is not going to be achieved while public services operate in a capitalist economy, for the reasons outlined in Chapter 6. But the struggle *for* control is important. This perspective provides a framework for different struggles on the quality and distribution of services, how they are organised and run, pay and conditions, their effectiveness and so on. It provides a means of connecting different campaigns, a basis for negotiation between workers and users, and a challenge to traditional trade union economism.

One aspect of the struggle for control is the workers' plans which have been developed by shop stewards' committees in several industrial firms. The idea of workers' plans was first developed by shop stewards at Lucas Aerospace. A questionnaire was distributed to workers asking them to make an audit of their job skills, plant and equipment and to put forward ideas for alternative products. Shop stewards then produced an Alternative Corporate Plan which included specification for about 150 socially useful products as an alternative to Lucas producing missiles and armaments. The plan helped shop stewards build a stronger combine committee and to stave off redundancies for several years despite strong opposition from the company and certain sections of the trade union movement. It also got the workers to be inventive and imaginative, using their skills and knowledge to think and develop different products. The plan was never implemented (although workers have helped finance the development of a road-rail bus outside of the company), but it did generate enthusiasm in the labour movement. Workers in Vickers, Dunlop and other companies have drawn together ideas for socially useful alternative production and products.

The idea of alternative plans is not new. For many years tenants' and residents' groups in redevelopment and improvement areas drew up plans for the future of their area. They often won, too.

Once we start applying such ideas to the public sector we cannot simply talk about workers' or trade union plans—alternative plans have to be based around workers' *and* users' needs and ideas. Workers' and users' plans within the public sector have the advantage that they bring together both producers and users in a common fight on both production issues, and the question of the use and control of the service or product.

Avoiding incorporation

Organisations, action and plans must be developed *independently* of the state. For state workers this poses many problems. Workers and users will have to struggle to retain this independence—to demand, negotiate and take action to get the state to implement *their* proposals. Much would be lost if councils simply expanded the production of goods and services without changing the way they are produced, run and controlled, or hived-off jobs and services to co-ops outside the public sector.

The response of the local state will vary depending on political control. Where there are currently the greatest opportunities (for example Sheffield, Greater London Council, West Midlands), there are also the greatest dangers. First, struggles could be incorporated. Involving workers and users in planning could be used as a diversion from campaigns over pay, conditions, cuts and the quality of services. There may be attempts to over-emphasise management's daily problems.

Ideology may become blurred. Whose ideas are they? Who is planning? Who is implementing the proposals? A shop stewards' committee which has developed proposals may find the authority claiming 'ownership' and credit for ideas. Some authorities may succumb to political pressure for 'successes' and therefore push workers and users to forgo the process of planning in order to get quick results.

The potential for building stronger labour movement organisations may be constrained. The leadership can be bought off by representation on committees and comfortable meetings in the town hall. There is also the problem of how workers within the state build up relationships with users who are 'outside' of it. Users may see workers negotiating and/or co-operating with management and councillors, but not see much happening directly in their interests or as a result of their action.

There is also a danger of some authorities encouraging participatory *popular* planning, but within existing structures, procedures and controls or by setting up new committees which are powerless to implement the plans. More could be achieved by concentrating support on a few organisations already tackling workers' and users' plans, and then generalising their experiences rather than by starting off from a 'let's all plan together' approach. 'Popular' initiatives may also raise false hopes and expectations of what 'planning' can deliver, or its effectiveness in stopping private sector plans. They may allow individuals more influence but stifle rank and file organising. People may get too ambitious for their ideas to succeed and lose sight of how important the process is.

Finally, control of services won't be handed over by management or councillors, but will have to be fought for through negotations, industrial and direct action. An effective system of industrial democracy and greater control in the planning and running of services can be achieved only by building and regaining strong, effective and independent organisations.

Going on the offensive

We have to move the terrain of the struggle away from concentrating on the cost of public services and the amount of public spending and to focus on the scale, quality and *effectiveness* of services. Failure to do so will mean fighting the Tories on their own ground. We *can't* win on the costs argument in isolation. This would mean throwing out all national agreements on wages and conditions and taking massive job and wage cuts. The very nature of privatisation, particularly given the current level of unemployment, means that the private sector will invariably undercut the public sector when it resorts to bidding on contracts. This does not mean ignoring inefficiency and waste. Nobody wants to pay higher rates and taxes than are necessary.

Privatisation is forcing groups of workers to go out and argue for their jobs, the value of the service they provide, and why it should be retained in the public sector. This has got to be taken further and not simply presented as a defence of jobs issue, which may lead to a greater degree of cynicism amongst users. This brings us back to how struggles are presented from the outset—simply concentrating on jobs and wages will draw limited support because, certainly in areas of high unemployment, it will be seen as a privileged section calling for support from those without jobs.

We need to develop new tactics to add a new dimension to traditional forms of industrial and community action in the public services. We have to make the scale, quality and availability of services more up front, include them in negotiating demands, and link them to pay and conditions. Industrial action in the public services affects users as well as industry and the state as employer. Success may well depend on developing and strengthening joint action with users of services and the extent to which industrial and community action is made overtly political.

We have to challenge the crazy way that public spending and borrowing is valued, measured, organised and allocated, and to get rid of notions that it is 'unproductive' and 'parasitic'. This means basing our arguments on socialist criteria about how *we* value and judge public services. These could include focusing on the range and quality of service, the degree of public accountability and control, the extent to which services provide socially useful work, the standard of pay and conditions and the knock-on effect of the service in the local and national economy.

We are now paying the penalty for the loss of vision in the labour movement. The Tories and their allies have a vision and know what they want. They mould policies and justify them to that end. There is virtually no socialist vision now publicly stated. Few argue 'this is what it could be like if . . . ' Instead they rely solely on policies which are expected to 'create jobs' and 'help the economy'.

Rank and file debate and discussion about the kind of housing, health and other services we want must be a priority. We have to go beyond slogans and figures and get down to people's needs and demands. Many people already have ideas about what services should be like, but need some stimulus to develop them. Let's start, for a change, with the kind of services we want; with good pay and conditions for workers; how we should *control* the services; the level, availability, quality and choice of services required; how a planned programme of investment and improvement could be implemented. Then we can work out what they will cost and how they can be financed, utilising all available resources.

There are examples of good practice on which to build and extend our ideas. Cheap bus fares in South Yorkshire, some good quality council housing, many well-equipped NHS health centres and hospitals and so on. We shouldn't focus simply on single issues like housing, health, or transport but also concentrate on **how services connect with each other**. We cannot develop a concept of what housing could be like without adequately dealing with child care, social facilities for the elderly, public transport to jobs, shops and entertainment. Satisfying different social needs will lead to **choice and variety** of services, many could not be provided by market forces. Identifying common interests must be another priority. Rather than focusing on the divisions between council tenants and owners we must concentrate on ways occupiers can gain control of their homes without ownership and exploitation. This will help to identify **class interests** and the need for class struggle.

Demands and ideas can be organised into those for immediate

implementation and longer term ones needed to transform services. We have to rebuild the belief that radical socialist alternatives **are** possible and feasible. Articulating the advantages of effective and efficient services giving choice and variety, with changed social relations in a socialist economy, is essential to seeing clearly the limits of existing public services, understanding the causes of these limitations, and developing organisations and action needed to transform services and the economy.

We must not be constrained by claims that there isn't any money to fund these changes. The vast resources in pension funds and insurance companies could be harnessed without damaging workers' longer term interests. The collection of deferred and unpaid company taxes, a wealth tax, and cuts in defence spending would produce billions of pounds.

What we need are more effective means of drawing together demands and ideas. Job monitoring and workers' and users' plans, described in Chapter 7, are two examples.

If we are to go on the offensive and win we need strong organisations at all levels. We need to improve trade unions in the public services, particularly in local government. Many areas still don't have joint shop stewards' committees (JSSCs) covering all departments. They are essential to prevent councils playing one department off against another, to unify different trade unions and to co-ordinate action. There is also an urgent need to combine committees to link up JSSCs and workers in similar departments in adjacent authorities. For example, Tyne and Wear DLO combine links shop stewards in DLOs in Newcastle, Gateshead, North and South Tyneside and Sunderland. They are also involved in the National DLO Combine. Far too much reliance is placed on joint consultative committees, on which both unions and management are represented, and on left Labour-controlled authorities and councillors. Anti-privatisation Committees could be set up by JSSCs, drawing in Trades Councils and users' organisations.

There is great scope for organising the users of services. There is already a wide range of organisations like tenants' associations, pensioners' groups, women's groups, unemployed workers' organisations and nursery action groups. Trades Councils play an important role in drawing together industrial and public sector trade unionists. Many already have strong links with local women's and tenants' organisations. Forming stronger links should become a priority. Single-issue campaigns should not be waged at the expense of support for other campaigns. The scale of privatisation and spending cuts means that a 'success' on one issue can be immediately wiped out by a defeat on another. Users' committees need to be organised in more public services, including transport and social services.

It is often very difficult to sustain national organisations of tenants and other users. Strictly local organisation and action have obvious limitations. Much greater commitment is needed to organisations like the National Housing Liaison Committee, which draws together tenants' groups, women's groups and trade union organisations campaigning on housing.

8.

How to Fight Privatisation

No single plan of action will defeat privatisation. The previous chapter spelt out a general labour movement strategy for the public services. This one puts forward detailed ideas for action against privatisation structured around a seven-point strategy. This is based on the premise that we can't and shouldn't try to tender alongside contractors. Public service jobs are not for sale. Nor should we rely solely on negotiating deals with management to retain direct labour. This often results in job and/or wage cuts. Instead, we have to campaign and negotiate for a good quality and wide range of services to meet social needs; decent pay, benefits and working conditions; and more worker and user control in running services. Contractors cannot compete on these terms. Privatisation can effectively be fought only by joint action both within and outside the workplace. It cannot be separated from the fight against the cuts nor the struggle to obtain a decent living wage.

Job and service monitoring

But before we can even look at the details of the strategy we need to be quite clear as to how we can keep abreast of changes in jobs and service provision. Some forms of privatisation are easy to identify. You can actually see new private hospitals or contractors taking over services. It is not so easy to spot the ways in which the NHS is being exploited for private health care, for example, the increasing use of NHS facilities for private patients. Developing a system of workers' and users' monitoring of jobs and services is very important. Monitoring can have a number of functions.

- First, it provides an early-warning system if privatisation or the closure of part of a service is threatened.
- Second, it helps workers to build up a clear picture of the existing use of contractors in their departments and to monitor their performances.
- Third, it helps workers to start to identify ways in which the service can be improved.

Monitoring could also be the workers' answer to work study. Jobs and services are usually scrutinised by management and work-study officers. This has intensified in recent years. With job monitoring, workers scrutinise what is going on around them in more detail and more systematically than they have done in the past. For example, workers could gather information about any general rundown in maintenance and repairs of buildings, equipment, transport, etc; examine staffing levels and changes in management attitudes; investigate changes in the level and quality of services; examine cuts in investment; draw together ideas and proposals to improve the service, increase its effectiveness, iron out current problems. and give more workers control over their jobs. It can be done by a small groups of shop stewards or branch members.

Another function of monitoring is to stop the use of public facilities for private use. ASTMS published some guidance notes and a checklist in *Medical World* (January/February 1982) which gives health workers ideas on how to monitor abuse of the NHS and to calculate the loss of fees. It points out that monitoring abuses of the NHS facilities is very difficult. It is the consultant who is ultimately responsible for notifying hospital authorities about the number of private patients using hospital services. However, ASTMS points to ways monitoring can be done and argues that waiting lists, standards of clinical care and services, laboratory tests, provision of accommodation and other areas of abuse should also be monitored.

Where contractors are employed, monitoring can check that they carry out the work fully and to the required standard. A system of monitoring private building contractors involved in re-pair and maintenance work on council housing has been devised in Sheffield. Monitoring by users could be extended to other services. Monitoring and information gathering is important, but it must never be at the expense of action. It can make workers and users aware of the fundamental threat of privatisation, and lay the basis for other forms of action under the seven-point strategy.

The seven-point strategy

The seven points are:
1. Developing alternative ideas and demands to improve services;
2. Education and propaganda;
3. Building stronger workplace organisations and links with workers in other boroughs;
4. Developing joint action and organising user committees with PTAs and tenants' groups;
5. Tactical use of industrial action and negotiating machinery;
6. Direct action by workers and users;
7. Counter offensive against contractors in public services.

The strategy was developed by NUPE London Divisional Local Government Area Committee following discussions by the Area Committee and Cuts Sub-committee assisted by Services to Community Action and Tenants (SCAT). It also draws on the experience of recent campaigns against privatisation.

The seven-point strategy is not a shopping list from which you can choose. Any campaign against privatisation must involve all seven elements of the strategy although the degree to which each is used will depend on local circumstances. No one tactic will win a struggle against contractors. This strategy can equally be used to fight the privatisation of local government services, the NHS, education, and nationalised industries.

Let us take each point in turn.

Developing alternatives to improve services

Alternative ideas and demands should play a major role in any campaign against privatisation. We need initiatives which will help to restore and build workers' confidence, and which will emphasise that workers and users have the right and ability to plan production and the delivery of services as much as management. But good ideas need money to implement them. It is therefore vital that we seek ways of gaining more control over how our money is invested by pension funds and insurance companies.

The increasing use of new technology in public services for communications, design, payrolls, information storage and management control is leading to big job losses. We need not only to develop better strategies to negotiate and control its introduction, but also to work out ways in which it can be used to improve services. Don't get caught in the trap of talking about 'efficiency' and 'value for money' aspects of the service which will be on management's terms. Instead, develop demands based on workers' and users' criteria—the need for the service to be *effective*. For instance:

- Are needs and priorities clearly identified?
- How can the service be made more effective, for example does it reach all those who want to use it and does the quality of service satisfy people's needs?
- How can wages, benefits and conditions be improved?
- How can the work be made more socially useful?
- How can it be linked to other key policies such as energy conservation?
- How can the improvements and expansion of servies be financed?

Local authority and nationalised industry pension funds have investments in companies now competing for council and NHS contracts. Workers are therefore helping to finance the takeover of their own or other workers' jobs. Trade unionists should demand that their pension funds sell their shares in companies privatising the health service and local council services and boycott all sales of shares in nationalised industries at the same time as proposing ways of reorganising services and changing certain procedures and practices. The way to make such change socially relevant is to place them in the context of other demands and proposals concerning the overall service.

Drawing up proposals to improve and expand services will require additional support and assistance from trade unions. The process of developing ideas and plans is just as important as the final set of proposals. This support will involve making services available to members and responding quickly to their requests for assistance and advice on technical, organising and campaigning matters. Officers and organisers are already overstretched dealing with pay negotiations, disputes and other trade union work. Public sector trade unions should urgently extend their research and education work by setting up resource units. They should draw on the experience of labour and community resource centres which have built up considerable experience in this field and directly support their work.

A 'plan' could range from a detailed charter of demands to a more comprehensive set of proposals covering different aspects of a service. Plans could cover the following, to varying degrees of detail:

- First, investment and resources. For example, the finance, labour, materials and other resources needed to improve and expand services, how they could be obtained, training needs, etc.
- Second, a production or service plan—how a particular service could be improved and reorganised to meet workers' and users' needs.
- Third, a use and organisation plan—which could include proposals for workers' and users' control of services and democratising management.
- Fourth, a plan of action—what kind of action is needed to get the proposals implemented and how the plan will be used as part of the wider struggle.

They should be seen as a means of drawing up negotiating demands. They are not just a collection of 'good ideas'. The process of planning and organising can enable workers and users to build confidence, strength and unity to take action to get demands implemented. These ideas and demands will form part of the development of both local and national alternative economic, political and social strategies. They are a means of getting the debate about alternative policies broadened out from the current concentration on generalised eonomic issues.

There is a danger that in the 'popularisation' of plans the original concept gets lost, distorted, or absorbed into the state's machinery, referred to in Chapter 7. It is therefore essential that we develop a strong set of criteria which can be rigorously applied to test the use, aims and possible benefits of such plans *before* they are initiated.

A workers' and users' plan could be based around a fight to retain jobs in a DLO and improve the repairs service. It could be developed jointly by shop stewards and representatives from the tenants' federations or associations. Information could be collected about the current and planned flow of work in the DLO, and the constraints imposed by the new legislation. Ideas could be drawn together for the issuing of job tickets and for decentralisation to area or estate-based teams. There could also be proposals to expand the production of items used in construction, such as furniture and fittings. Wider housing issues (such as the kind of housing we want and provision of child care and community facilities as an integral part of housing) would constitute an important element of this type of plan. The plan would provide a basis for joint action by workers and tenants.

Education and propaganda

This section gives some idea for disseminating information to other workers, to users of services and to the wider public. It means using the existing newsletters and bulletins of labour movement organisations; the local press, radio and television; specifically organised educational workshops; and special leaflets, posters and stickers.

Workplace leaflets
Use existing newsletters and specially prepared leaflets to back up branch and mass meetings. They should include details of the inferior wages, conditions and benefits, the effects on standards and control of the service, and the likely loss of jobs if the service is privatised. The advantages of public service should also be stated.

Explain the reasons for any lack of service; the effects of the spending cuts; why you are unhappy with standards. Management and councillors may be wanting to reduce standards and increase complaints in order to help pave the way for privatisation. Also explain what the authority is trying to do and the tactics it uses.

Counter contractors' claims about how they can improve efficiency and achieve a more economical use of public money.

Argue against workers buying shares if you work for a state company which is being sold off. Argue that real control will rest with the financial institutions. Argue that workers could be more secure placing their savings elsewhere. (At the same time, it might be useful for the JSSC to buy the minimum number of shares in order to gain access to the annual general meeting and usual shareholders' information.) Counter any propaganda about worker buy-outs: they are in reality management buy-outs.

Positive slogans rather than 'Defend . . . ' could be prepared for posters. Put them on all the authority's premises and vehicles as well as the usual places. Don't wait until privatisation is threatened.

As soon as you hear that the authority is preparing an evaluation or reorganisation report on a particular service, prepare your own propaganda.

Workplace meetings, shop stewards' training and information

and educational material for members play a more important role in the public sector because workers are often dispersed. Building workers, home helps, and other workers usually work in small groups or individually and rarely meet as a workforce. Organising strategies must take this into account and demand more time off for meetings. Shop stewards' training should include more organising and campaigning work.

Leaflets to users

Parks, refuse, cleansing and some other services are provided for everyone on a regular basis. Other services, such as social services, home helps, and residential care for the elderly, are provided for particular groups of people on a regular basis. Services such as health care are commonly used only when needed. Some services are taken to the home, others require people to go to them. Some workers operate from public buildings, others from office blocks. All these differences have to be borne in mind when writing leaflets and organising their distribution. In some cases, most of the public don't know the scale and quality of services provided until they have to use them. It may be necessary to prepare one leaflet for users and another for the wider public.

Leaflets and information should be written by and for women who work in the service and those who use it. They should explain what the service does. For example, home helps don't just do cleaning, as some ratepayers' groups claim, but also shop and deal with health, personal and family matters. Argue that the cost of services is only one criterion—more important is its effectiveness in meeting needs.

Leaflets should also explain the consequences of privatisation for both users and workers, its effects on the level and quality of the service.

Explain the advantages of the public service and its achievements. Argue that the workers themselves want to see services improved and expanded and invite users to contribute ideas and comments on how this could be done.

Publicise the failures of privatisation. For example, CK Coaches going bust in Cardiff, massive increases in BUPA health insurance, Pritchard's fines in Wandsworth for not cleaning streets, contractors losing contracts. You could add material collected during job monitoring. This must be part of a wider strategy to destabilise and discredit particular firms. Also include information about firms' activities in other countries, covering exploitation of workers, corruption scandals, botched work, and soaring costs.

Take particular aspects of public services to highlight and co-ordinate propaganda and action around them. Build on this support to argue for other services and the principles of public service. Argue against profiteering from any service.

General leaflets could be produced for widespread distribution, but each workplace should be encouraged to produce its own material. More workers can be involved and leaflets can be aimed at specific groups of users.

It's one thing to produce leaflets—it's another to get them effectively distributed. Keep pressing other workers to distribute them and ask for report-backs on progress, reaction, etc., at stewards' and branch meetings. Ask Trades Councils, Tenants' Federations, Community Health Councils, local Labour Parties and other organisations to distribute leaflets through their mailings.

Education workshops

Organise workshops using the material in the NUPE education pack or this book. Educationals can be a key way of drawing people into action. You may want to hold workshops which draw active members of other unions fighting privatisation and invite representatives from other organisations to participate.

Building stronger workplace organisations

The previous chapter argued that in taking on multinational companies it was essential that the trade union movement built unity and co-operation between unions, organised joint shop stewards' committees and combines throughout the public services, as well as developing strong international links at all levels. It is also essential that these organisations involve the rank and file membership. It is the membership which has to be convinced that services can be improved and more control gained over jobs and services by retaining them within the public sector. This means it is necessary to organise regular depot/section/department mass meetings as soon as privatisation is threatened. Don't wait until you get clarification from the authority—this may take weeks, which gives management and the contractor time to spread their propaganda. Regular leaflets or bulletins to the workforce are also essential. You will have to convince workers that working for a contractor is not going to benefit them.

Work out and publicise the effects of privatisation for other workers and departments including central services. Explain how their jobs will be affected, for example fewer wages to prepare, less supplies to order. Get over to management that they are threatened as well—make them uncertain. Show that other workers' jobs, job opportunites and their use of services are threatened.

If you don't already have any sympathetic links in management, try to establish them. Discreet exchange of information will help to alert you to any planned reorganisation proposals or preparation of tender documents. If the authority refuses to release information, then go to the press to put pressure on them.

Many workers in the public services work alone or in small groups, such as home helps, street cleaners, park and garden workers, and may see each other only once a week. It is therefore very important to try to have the maximum number of union meetings in worktime that the authority permits and to try to reach agreement to extend it. Make a special effort to help to organise and support these workers.

Regular departmental shop stewards' committee and anti-privatisation committee meetings are essential to get a clear idea of what is happening, to discuss strategies and to organise and co-ordinate inter-union action. Make links with JSSCs in other authorities and cities, and invite speakers from those JSSCs who already have experience of fighting privatisation.

Line up speakers at branch meetings and encourage members to attend—make sure they know when and where meetings are held. Have full report-backs and discussion about the privatisation campaign.

Get a mandate from the membership for immediate industrial action if anyone is victimised by management for implementing action against privatisation.

Support local authority and other public sector workers in dispute in other areas. Consider taking action against the same contractor(s) if they are involved in your area. Keep members fully informed about what is happening in disputes in neighbouring areas—it could cause splits in your own ranks if they are confronted by pickets when they know nothing about the dispute.

Tighten your own control of the job by ensuring that standards of work are maintained—you can't afford to leave it to management. This is not doing management's job for them, but workers taking control of standards or work and establishing their control over maintaining them. This could increase morale and confidence and minimise councillors' and management's attacks.

Identify areas and issues on which joint action between different unions could be agreed. Even if there has been conflict and lack of unity in previous disputes it's important to get over bitterness. Privatisation cannot be fought alone.

Try to get your union to organise unemployed workers' sections and/or direct support for unemployed action groups. It is vital to retain contact with members, in particular women workers, after they leave the job. They usually leave the union and become lost and forgotten in unpaid domestic labour with even less time to be involved in labour movement organisations.

Developing joint action and user committees

The response to privatisation by labour movement users of services has been very patchy. Apart from the support given to workers in the campaigns noted above, most action has centred on council house sales. Occupations and other direct action have delayed, but not stopped, sales in various cities. Much of the potential for widespread action dwindled in 1980 after Labour councils ducked out of collective opposition to the government when the Housing Act came into force. Nevertheless, recently a 'Stop the Sale Campaign' has organised action to prevent Glasgow council selling the Hutchesontown and other estates. Trades Councils have initiated and supported many campaigns. For example, Basingstoke Trades Council recently helped to organise demonstrations by refuse workers and opposition to a new private hospital. They also organised six educationals on privatisation. However, much more needs to be done.

Experience has clearly shown that joint action won't just come about because it is a good idea—it has to be worked for. Don't wait for other unions or tenants' and community organisations to contact you, whether over your own or their struggles—take the initiative and, if you don't succeed at first, keep trying. Links take time to build. There are many examples of initial rebuffs later resulting in joint action.

You will have to go out and argue why there should be joint action and unity, and explain the benefits and reasons. Argue that the ultimate causes of problems at work, at home and in the public services are often the same, that we share the same interests: we all need housing, health and education. Show with examples that we need to share experience and information and learn new tactics. Last but not least that we need to heal divisions which only weaken and sap our strength.

You will have to tackle inbuilt ideas about the workplace, the job, and trade unions. People have a home-life and use services—but they tend to see the three activities as separate. This means going beyond traditional trade union concerns such as wages and conditions, and fighting to break down deep divisions and resentments.

People have little real opportunity to vent opinions, anger and resentments about how public services are run, how people behave to make public service workers' jobs harder. Consequently, initial meetings are likely to be quite aggressive. It is important to persevere through these meetings—experience shows that once people vent their anger and begin to understand the workers' or users' views then there is a real basis for developing a working relationship.

It is vital that links between workers and users go well beyond a few activists. Although links may start through a few individuals, it is important that more people become involved in attending joint meetings and that both sides receive full report-backs.

Joint action won't happen just through education and propaganda and passing strongly worded resolutions. There has to be active and material support for each other's struggles—go on pickets, support mass meetings and demonstrations.

There may be some situations where there are major conflicts of interest and/or strong political differences between workers and users, and between trade union and community organisations, which will prevent any working relationship from developing.

It was pointed out in the previous chapter that the labour movement hasn't really gained or even fought for increased control of public services. In most public services there are no users' committees. Users' committees in some of the nationalised industries, for example, the Post Office, are remote, toothless national bodies. Participation in planning in the late 1960s and early 1970s was, not surprisingly, essentially about 'consultation exercises' on the state's terms. They were far removed from any notion of people having any real control over their environment. Similarly, the 'new' interest in decentralisation of services *could* be a means of gaining more control. However, there is nothing in decentralisation which makes more worker and user control more inevitable—in fact, it can easily lead to illusions of more control when power is even more centralised and local offices are left to implement policies with fewer and fewer resources.

A strategy to fight privatisation has to include a perspective and a campaign to fight for control of services at different levels. But control has to be fought for; it is a political battle to wrest power from the state and the interests it serves.

Initial links between workers and users could develop into a permanent working relationship without necessarily forming any organisational links. In some situation, joint tenants' and workers' or workers' and users' committees have been set up or a number of organisations have collectively set up a particular campaign. For example, the Kentish Town Health Centre Users' Group was started in 1977, when staff invited representatives from local community groups and users of the centre to meet to discuss whether services needed to be changed or improved. The users' group helps to keep up the standards of the centre, handles complaints by patients and provides a way for people to put forward their ideas.

Another example is in Hackney where, in 1981, a committee of tenants and DLO shop stewards was set up to examine the problems of repairs and maintenance on council estates. They produced a report which included recommendations to have estate/area-based repairs teams, planned maintenance and cyclical repair, reorganisation of management and procedures for dealing with repairs, and replacing the bonus system with proper salaries. A review body within the DLO has worked closely with stewards and a number of recommendations have been implemented.

There is scope for much more joint action and establishment of permanent links between union branches and shop stewards' committees and community organisations. Examples could include links between parks and gardens shop stewards and local tenants' groups, play groups and nursery campaigns to petition for better facilities in parks, and supervised play areas. Recreation and sports centres could set up workers' and users' committees to monitor use of the centre and recommend improvements, and to link up with unemployed action groups or centres to campaign for free or reduced rates.

Tactical use of industrial action and negotiating machinery

Industrial action alone will not stop privatisation. It must be used as a means of strengthening a negotiating position and indicating to the authority that it will have to fight to implement privatisation. Because of the nature of many public service jobs, particularly in health and social services, many members are naturally reluctant to take traditional strike action. They have a close relationship with the people they provide the service for. Many people are not prepared to take action on the basis that there is very little wrong with the service and that the public will not support industrial action. Industrial action which alienates a large number of users and the wider public can be counterproductive in fighting privatisation. The authority could readily use this alienation to further isolate the workforce.

Industrial action should be co-ordinated with other forms of action. Before embarking on industrial action, carefully work out the consequences for workers in other departments—will they support the action even if they lose bonus or overtime?

Of course, industrial action in both the public and private sectors has political and economic dimensions to varying degrees. The economic effects of industrial action in the public sector are often overstated. Strikes in transport and communications don't halt production, only distribution, and employers and workers usually use alternative forms of transport. Only in the energy field can industrial action halt production. Public sector workers can also stop financial transactions both into the state (rates and taxes) and payments from the state to the private sector. Pulling out computer staff may hit payments to local firms and rate collection, but it also hits the wages to other workers in the same public body. Selectivity requires a greater class consciousness.

Here are some examples of different forms of action.

As soon as there is a hint of use of contractors, try to get NALGO, ASTMS, or other white-collar unions to refuse to co-operate with the preparation of tenders, legal advice, letters, advertising and so on. NALGO action of this type in Bury prevented the council from privatising the Public Services Department. It is not enough to rely on branch resolutions. Some officers may ignore them and continue to preparing the ground for contractors. Unions will have to encourage and support the implementation of each other's policies.

Strike action could include industrial action by a department threatened with privatisation, and/or selected action by other sections to maximise the economic and political impact on the authority. Or there could be all-out industrial action. Each situation is different, politically and historically, but a number of lessons have been learnt.

● First, each section and department must fully understand all the facts about the threat of privatisation and must be willing to support, both politically and financially, those sections or departments taking action.

● Second, the initial strategy must include ways and means of escalating the action. The response to the use of scab labour, victimisation and other action by the authority must be worked out beforehand.

● Third, strike action must be *part* of a campaign and linked to other action, such as education and propaganda, and direct action by users.

● Fourth, action must be supported nationally by other unions in neighbouring authorities or other parts of the service.

● Fifth, whenever possible, counter measures should be taken to minimise the effect on working-class users.

● Sixth, the strike action should be co-ordinated and involve as many workers as possible with regular report-backs.

Agreements for 'no compulsory redundancy' are important. They can also effectively put up the cost of privatisation if the authority cannot redeploy workers. But don't feel secure behind them. An authority can still make a 'no compulsory redundancy agreement' *and* privatise several services.

Co-operate with management consultants only if the work cannot be done internally and there are specific advantages in the use of consultants. Demand to see their terms of reference. Also try to reach agreement with the authority that the unions should have copies of the draft and final reports, the right to submit their own evidence, and that nothing will be implemented without agreement with the unions. Refuse to co-operate with the authority's own work study officers unless such agreements are reached. Otherwise refuse to supply information or give access to the job.

Devise selective industrial action to highlight the threat of privatisation. This could include cutting off or reducing services to private industry, business and selected areas for certain periods while maintaining or improving services (to show what they could be like) to working-class areas. Organise open days (the Fire Brigade already do this) to show the importance of the service and its effectiveness, how the service would be affected by privatisation. Link this in with local festivals and events. Also organise and publicise workers' visits to other authorities' services, or to your own, to publicise improvements, and standards of work.

Refuse to cover vacant or frozen posts and demand more staff. Don't deal with this as an internal matter because all the public will see is the work not being done and possible deterioration of the service. Don't cover up for cuts—expose them. Explain the causes and consequences of vacant posts in leaflets, letters to the press and at public meetings.

Refuse to collect increased charges for services, but continue to provide the service.

Boycott voluntary workers who are being used to undermine or replace paid workers. Also boycott all co-operation with local voluntary bodies working with the council to supply volunteers. Refuse to process their applications for grants. Find out if other labour movement organisations have representatives on these voluntary organisations' committees and get them to start internal opposition.

Direct action by workers and users

Direct action can play a key role in a campaign: it helps to build political support, threatens loss of support for the opposition, and causes further disruption of privatisation proceeds. It can also be used to actually prevent or delay the takeover of a service by a contractor.

The success of direct action by workers and users will depend, in part, on the kind of links and working relationships established with community-based and other organisations in the labour movement, as well as on education and propaganda work.

Before deciding on any action it would be useful to examine the following questions:
- What effect will it have politically. Will it make it more difficult to privatise—if so, how?
- Can other aims be achieved by taking this particular action?
- What effect will it have politically? Will it make it more difficult
- Will it be divisive with other workers?
- What other supporting action can be taken?

- Can it be sustained/completed, will enough people take part and will it draw in more people to the campaign?
- What is the likely response of the authority and how can you counter-respond?
- How can the action take place at the most advantageous time?
- What kind of follow-up action can be taken?

How well things are organised is just as important as the *kind* of action you take. The following are some ideas for different forms of action.

Picket and lobby council meetings as soon as there is a threat of privatisation or use of consultants—and continue to picket at every subsequent meeting when the issue is to be discussed. Use your existing network of contacts in the labour movement to get people to attend. Link up education and propaganda work to call for wider support at later pickets. Always try to have leaflets to hand out to councillors, supporters and the public.

Organise boycotts urging workers not to use private bus companies or private health care facilities. Urge reciprocal action by other unions. This means extending the type of tactics used against Barclays Bank involvement in South Africa to other companies. The 12 million membership of trade unions represents a massive 'consumer market' in Britain and we should use this powerful position much more effectively.

Whenever possible, marches and demonstrations should be jointly organised or sponsored with other labour movement organisations to ensure maximum support. Think of other forms of action before planning a march—sometimes it is too 'easy' to resort to the traditional form of action when other types of action might be more successful.

Linking action to strikes provides a way in which people can show support. It can also be a means of involving those on strike to turn up on picket lines. Action could include demonstrations, a mass picket of a particular council building, mass leafleting of shopping and residential areas, or pre-emptive action to stop people 'taking it out' on the workers.

Occupations/work-ins can vary from the short-term occupation of specific buildings or offices to the longer-term work-in (Hounslow, Elizabeth Garrett Anderson, St. Benedicts and other hospitals adopted this tactic in their fight against closure).

Campaigns against the building of new private facilities could involve: lobbying and action to force planning applications to public inquiry: preparing and submitting alternative plans for the use of the site: occupation of buildings on the site to prevent demolition; and the blacking of sites by building workers.

Declare workers' and users' control of a particular area, service or building. For example, workers, tenants and residents could declare control of refuse/cleansing in an area to highlight the need for improvements, or to implement agreed (by workers and tenants) changes in working practices and methods. This is a good way of demonstrating unity and the need for public service.

Organise a campaign to improve services. Carry out surveys, prepare reports and leaflets to take the initiative away from the authorities and their focus on the costs of services. The aim would be to force a public debate about which existing needs are not being met, and how public service workers are committed to fighting for improvements.

Refuse to pay/collect rent and other increased charges. This has to be well organised as workers may be victimised by management. Users have to know its purpose and be involved. It must be linked to other action.

Set up a workers' and users' public inquiry into the service which could cover needs, resources, improvements, control, and management. Arrange for labour movement organisations to be represented on a small panel to take evidence from a wide range of labour and community organisations.

Organise demonstrations to stop the transfer of public equipment, patients, and buildings to private use. This may occur as a preliminary to contractors taking over. Alternatively release a dossier on the shoddy work and cost overruns by contractors.

Picket or hold a demonstration at the Stock Exchange, company AGM, banks financing a contractor's expansion to take over services, as part of a strategy to try to destabilise a company.

Contact workers in other local authorities whose pension funds are investing in contractors. Seek their support.

Counter offensive against contractors in public services

There could be three parts to a counter offensive:
- fighting the preparation of tenders:
- imposing strict conditions on contractors and
- campaigning to remove contractors from public services.

Fighting the preparation of tenders

As soon as there is any threat of privatisation it is vital to ensure that any further debate and negotiation are based on the principles of public service, the level and the quality of services and that any comparison between public service and private firms must compare like with like. Don't get sucked into the dangerous trap of simply arguing who can do the job more cheaply.

Privatisation is often preceded by the use of management consultants investigating the efficiency and organisation of services. It is important to take action with other unions to agree and implement a policy of non-co-operation with consultants—refuse access to premises and information. At the very least, this could slow down the authority's plans and give you more time to organise a campaign. Ensure that any information and figures the consultants do get are accurate and reflect the full range and quality of the service.

It is important to argue that the cost of the service is only one criterion and must be considered alongside effectiveness, quality, and the degree to which needs are met. The Treasury, supported by the House of Commons Public Accounts Committee, has issued new 'value for money' guidelines for public sector organisations purchasing supplies. 'Value for money should not be judged solely on the basis of the lowest initial cost. Design, reliability and maintainability, for example, will affect the total cost over the life of a product'. These arguments can equally be used within the public sector.

Any financial comparisons which are made must compare like with like. Don't get drawn into comparing vague 'bid' prices from contractors with detailed costings of direct labour. Make sure that *all* costs of the service are taken into account. These would include the costs of providing the same level and quality of service; the cost of maintaining the same standard of work and quality of materials; and the costs of consultants, lawyers and others involved in preparing tenders and contracts. There are also the costs to the authority for all supervision (staff and all their overheads) of the contractor and enforcement of statutory obligations, and environmental health standards. Additional charges may be made by the contractor direct to the users of the service. The costs of extending the service to new housing areas, and facilities, should be included. The capital costs of returning the work to the authority when the contract is terminated could be substantial.

Imposing strict conditions on contractors
This will cost the contractor money and that means tenders will be higher than they would otherwise have been. Local authorities, the NHS, nationalised industries and government departments have set procedures and conditions which lay down the basis on which contractors have to tender. Try to strengthen these Standing Orders or Codes of Practice. The Local Government Act 1972 (Section 135) gives local authorities the power to draw up Standing Orders but it is up to the authority and not the contractor to ensure that the Standing Orders have been complied with. An authority's failure to enforce the Standing Orders does not invalidate a contract.

Authorities or particular departments who use contractors a lot often have an approved list of contractors who are invited to tender for particular jobs. This list should be as short as possible and should include only those contractors who have clearly demonstrated their ability to meet all the conditions in the Standing Orders. Conditions should cover wages, health and safety, trade union recognition and negotiation, apprentice training, subcontracting, supervision and other items. Examples of conditions include the following.

Contractors must fully comply with the Health and Safety at Work Act 1974 and submit an acceptable policy statement on how they intend to implement it in the contract, ensure that there are properly recognised and elected safety reps, and permit the council's Chief Safety Adviser to inspect all parts of the site at any time. They must also employ a reasonable proportion of craft apprentices genuinely receiving training.

Contractors should be subject to penalty clauses for inadequate standards or non-completion of service. The contractor must also post a substantial performance payment and guarantee bond for the term of the contract. Conditions are one thing. Implementing them is another. So it is crucial to ensure that the authority has the resources and political commitment to carry out constant supervision of contract clauses. This means having adequately trained staff to supervise work, carry out spot checks on contractors' work and investigate complaints.

There must be regular reporting to council committees so that any necessary action against contractors can be authorised. Trade unions should secure the right of disclosure of information about any contractor tendering or doing work for the authority, together with details of breaches of Standing Orders.

Sheffield council have recently started monitoring the work and standards of private contractors involving the Public Works Shop Stewards' Committee and the Tenants' Federation. Tenants and workers are supplied with leaflets explaining key sections of the Standing Orders, together with phone numbers of inspectors, officers and councillors if they consider contractors are failing to implement the Orders or to maintain standards.

Campaigning to remove contractors from public services

It is crucial constantly to monitor the scale of contracting out, the performance of contractors, and the implementation of conditions on contractors.

If contractors take over you could take immediate industrial action until they are removed, or alternatively adopt a policy of non-co-operation by refusing any assistance or advice, refusing to allow them the use of the authority's equipment, refusing to finish off any work done by contractors until the authority gives a commitment not to use contractors on similar work again, and/or refusing to work alongside contract labour.

While these tactics may well succeed in clawing back into the authority work recently allocated to contractors, they will have only limited effect in getting rid of contractors who regularly carry out work for the authority. Industrial action and non-co-operation can be effective if the authority has the resources immediately to carry out the work itself. In many situations this is not possible. It is therefore essential to work out ways in which the authority could obtain the resources, equipment and expertise to do the work itself. This could involve investigating whether other departments in the authority could undertake the work or combining together all the similar contracted-out work from different departments which might be more viable than an individual department doing it. Also explore the possibility of entering into a consortium with neighbouring authority/ies to share the cost and use of expensive equipment, such as road asphalt machines, the bulk purchase of materials, or the joint production of commonly used items.

Investigate whether there are resources—staff, equipment and plant—not being fully utilised at present within the authority, together with additional resources needed (such as retraining re-quirements of existing or new staff) where additional finance could be obtained.

Investigate the 'peaks and troughs' of the authority's workload, particularly in professional and technical work. There may be ways of changing or re-ordering work to reduce variations in workload and the need to use private firms. It is also important to identify new areas of work, and also work currently done by the private sector, which could be done by the public services.

Another tactic is to try to unionise workers employed by contractors. This will usually be difficult because, even though contractors often claim they have 'no objection' to attempts to unionise and that workers have a 'free choice' the reality is something different. Intimidation and threats about loss of jobs and a total lack of trade union facilities makes organising difficult.

It is important in seeking recruits that the branch and officials aren't content with simply recruiting members as part of a numbers game. It must be a tactic which is part of a wider strategy to improve and expand public services. To this end recruitment is a tactic to help in the longer-term strategy to get the work returned within the authority.

Union membership will lead to improved conditions for the workforce, less victimisation of individuals and support for any industrial action. Recruitment should also be part of a strategy to destabilise firms through co-ordinated industrial action in different areas where the same company is operating.

Privatisation poses a new challenge to the labour movement. The previous narrow focus on wages and conditions, slogans about public ownership and general ownership and general demands for more services have caught up with us. The very existence of the welfare state and public services is now at stake. Harnessing workers' and users' ideas, skills and power in a struggle for control of public services and the economy is the only way forward.

A Guide to Reading

Chapter 2

Information about which services are threatened or being privatised comes from a number of sources. Trade union journals are very useful, such as NUPE's *Public Employees*, NALGO's *Public Service*, SCPS's *Opinion*, TGWU's *Record*, UCATT's *Viewpoint* and COHSE's *Health Service*. The *Financial Times*, the *Guardian*, *The Times*, *Morning Star* and the *Economist* are also valuable sources. Papers and journals such as the *New Statesman*, *Socialist Challenge*, *Socialist Worker*, *Tribune*, *Labour Herald*, *Labour Research*, and *Community Action* report regularly on the scale of privatisation and struggles against it. An anti-privatisation newsletter, *Public Service Action*, from Services to Community Action and Tenants, 31 Clerkenwell Close, London EC1, covers a wide range of services. The TUC Educational Service produced a compilation of cuttings in its Stage 2 education pack in 1982. The Tory Party now issues an annual *Privatisation Directory*. An analysis of public spending cuts and contracting out in America is contained in *Crisis in the Public Sector*, Union for Radical Political Economics, New York, 1981.

Chapter 3

The Tenth Report from the Committee of Public Accounts, House of Commons, 1982 examined the financial details of the sale of BP, British Aerospace, Cable and Wireless, and Amersham International. See also David Philip's article 'Great Britain Incorporated', *New Statesman*, 29 October 1982.

Chapter 4

Right-wing organisations mentioned in the text regularly bring out reports arguing for more privatisation.

Information on contractors can be obtained from company annual reports and the monthly journal *Labour Research*. The NUPE London Division education pack *Improve Public Services: Shut Out Contractors* has a section on how to investigate companies.

Chapter 5

The effects of privatisation on British Telecom are set out in the POEU's *British Telecom: Privatisation Evidence presented to the Department of Industry*, 1982, the Union of Communication Workers' *The Privatisation of British Telecom*, 1982, together with Counter Information Services' *Private Line: The Future of British Telecom*, 1982.

The consequences of the growth of private health are well documented in *Going Private*, Fightback and Politics of Health Group, 1981 and Steve Iliffe's *Condition Critical*, Communist Party, 1982. A number of useful memoranda and briefings have been issued by NHS Unlimited, c/o Frank Dobson MP.

A number of trade unions contributed to *Privatisation*, Occasional Paper No. 86, Trade Union Research Unit, Ruskin College. This covers both the effects of privatisation on employment and services and the scale of contracting out.

Information on job losses and contractors' wages and conditions can usually be obtained from council committee reports prepared immediately prior to a decision to privatise or not. A pamphlet by the General and Municipal Workers' Union, *Privatisation and Public Services*, 1982, is also useful in this context. So too is *Public or Private: the case against privatisation*, Labour Research Department, 1982.

The effects of the sale of council housing are documented in *The Great Sales Robbery*, Services to Community Action and Tenants, 1980.

Chapter 6

Unfortunately there is no one source which gives an analysis of services in the nineteenth century and traces their eventual takeover by the state. *Building with Direct Labour*, Conference of Socialist Economists, 1978 and *Direct Building*, Labour Research Department, 1929 are essential reading on direct labour organisations. David Widgery, *Health in Danger*, Macmillan, 1979 and Colin Thunhurst, *It Makes You Sick: The Politics of the NHS*, Pluto Press, 1982 remind us of health care conditions before the NHS was set up. A history of council housing can be found in *Community Action* No. 24, Feb–March 1976 and *Whatever Happened to Council Housing*, Community Development Projects, 1976. The development of electricity and gas services can be found in Leslie Hannah, *Electricity Before Nationalisation*, Macmillan, 1979; and Malcolm Peebles, *Evolution of the Gas Industry*, Macmillan, 1980. Derek Aldcroft and Harry Richardson cover the development of railways in their book *The British Economy 1870–1939*, Macmillan, 1969.

A discussion of the contradictions experienced working in and using public services is contained in the London–Edinburgh Weekend Return Group's *In and Against the State*, Pluto Press, 1980. Peter Fairbrother's *Working for the State*, Workers' Educatiional Association, 1982 is equally useful.

The case for public services is made clearly and convincingly in David Hall, *The Cuts Machine: The Politics of Public Expenditure*, Pluto Press, 1983.

Chapters 7 and 8

The two educational packs by NUPE, *Improve Public Services: Shut Out Contractors* by the London Division and *Keep Services Public* by the national office have detailed ideas for organising and action.

Birmingham and Bury NALGO branches issued regular anti-privatisation newsletters as part of their struggle against contractors and consultants.

Job and service monitoring, together with workers' and users' plans, are further explained in a forthcoming report from Services to Community Action and Tenants.